## ALSO BY DAVID MAMET

### NONFICTION:

*Recessional: The Death of Free Speech
and the Cost of a Free Lunch*
*The Secret Knowledge: On the Dismantling of American Culture*
*South of the Northeast Kingdom*
*Jafsie and John Henry*
*Make-Believe Town*
*A Whore's Profession*
*On Directing Film*
*True and False: Heresy and Common Sense for the Actor*
*Three Uses of the Knife*
*Theatre*
*Bambi vs. Godzilla: On the Nature, Purpose,
and Practice of the Movie Business*
*The Wicked Son: Anti-Semitism, Self-Hatred, and the Jews*
*Writing in Restaurants*
*The Cabin: Reminiscences and Diversions*
*Some Freaks*

### FICTION:

*The Village*
*The Old Religion*
*Wilson: A Consideration of the Sources*
*Three War Stories*
*The Diary of a Porn Star*
*Chicago*

# EVERYWHERE
# AN OINK OINK

## An Embittered, Dyspeptic, and Accurate Report of Forty Years in Hollywood

# DAVID MAMET

## With Illustrations by the Author

**SIMON & SCHUSTER**
New York  London  Toronto  Sydney  New Delhi

Simon & Schuster
1230 Avenue of the Americas
New York, NY 10020

First Simon & Schuster hardcover edition December 2023

SIMON & SCHUSTER and colophon are registered trademarks of Simon & Schuster, Inc.

For information about special discounts for bulk purchases, please contact Simon &
Schuster Special Sales at 1-866-506-1949 or business@simonandschuster.com.

The Simon & Schuster Speakers Bureau can bring authors to your live event. For more
information or to book an event, contact the Simon & Schuster Speakers Bureau at
1-866-248-3049 or visit our website at www.simonspeakers.com.

*Interior design by Carly Loman*

Manufactured in the United States of America

10  9  8  7  6  5  4  3  2  1

Library of Congress Cataloging-in-Publication Data

Names: Mamet, David, author.
Title: Everywhere an oink oink : an embittered, dyspeptic, and accurate report of forty years
   in Hollywood / by David Mamet ; with illustrations by the author.
Description: First Simon & Schuster hardcover edition. | New York : Simon and Schuster,
   2023. | Includes index.
Identifiers: LCCN 2023013998 (print) | LCCN 2023013999 (ebook) | ISBN 9781668026311
   (hardcover) | ISBN 9781668026328 (paperback) | ISBN 9781668026335 (ebook)
Subjects: LCSH: Mamet, David. | Dramatists, American—20th century—Biography. |
   Dramatists, American—21st century—Biography. | Motion picture producers and
   directors—United States—Biography. | Screenwriters—United States—Biography.
Classification: LCC PS3563.A4345 Z46 2023 (print) | LCC PS3563.A4345 (ebook) |
   DDC 812/.54 [B]—dc23/eng/20230623
LC record available at https://lccn.loc.gov/2023013998
LC ebook record available at https://lccn.loc.gov/2023013999

ISBN 978-1-6680-2631-1
ISBN 978-1-6680-2633-5 (ebook)

This book is dedicated to R. J. Pidgeon.

Mr. Michael Johnson was a man of a large and robust body, and of a strong and active mind; yet, as in the most solid rocks veins of unsound substance are often discovered, there was in him a mixture of that disease, the nature of which eludes the most minute enquiry, though the effects are well known to be a weariness of life, an unconcern about those things which agitate the greater part of mankind, and a general sensation of gloomy wretchedness.

—James Boswell, *The Life of Samuel Johnson, LL.D.*

# CONTENTS

# CONTENTS

# EVERYWHERE
## AN OINK OINK

# PROLOGUE:
## FORTY YEARS IN A HAREM

I am willing to think ill of anyone, so I suppose I have an open mind.

It was easy to abominate the liars and fools who were the Producer Coterie of my youth; but in defense not of them but of our Culture, everyone then knew everyone was lying.

The starry-eyed got off the bus and believed or accepted the bushwa until they had been seduced and abandoned, perhaps serially. They then tried to share their wisdom with the new arrivals, to as little avail as reasoning with a lovestruck youth, or a stone.

But with the fall of the Other Shoes, the situation was eventually seen to have been screaming out its clarity:

Producer: "I love you and everything you've ever done."

Aspirant: "Pay my rent."

Producer: "Lie on the bed and think of England."

Cheap literature was full of tales of the Gentleman Robber, but the Gentleman Mugger was nowhere a staple of Romance.

It's an axiom that if each man acted in his Own Best Interest this would be a paradise on earth. But who has ever understood another's Best Interest as other than that which would (coincidentally) benefit *oneself*?

The whole profit in the sugarcane is in the last two inches. Those who do not cut it close to the ground will fall to the mercantile wisdom of those who do. The Talented here may stand in for the sugarcane.

The producers shot Judy Garland full of speed, just as the canny restaurant owner, paying rent twenty-four hours a day, keeps the restaurant working through the night. Just like Judy.

*   *   *

We know that culture beats organization every time. In Hollywood there is no organization—it has always been the war of each against all.

Sporadic efforts at organization, here as elsewhere, are only collusion; that is, the momentary association of brigands against their mutual prey. As everywhere, the collusive entity dissolves when one element or individual sees the possibility of usurping the communal gain.

Absent a communal culture, even organized religion, like representative government, devolves into conspiracy against its constituents. But though Hollywood lacks an organization it possesses a culture.

Like that of aviation, it grows from the one immutable fact: in aviation, that on every flight the flyer risks his life; in Hollywood, that everyone is flogging nonsense.

There is little difference in the assumption that the earth is burning or that Mickey Mouse is funny. Those who hold the high ground exhort or extort agreement. In the case of the mouse they do so with that false smile that always indicates duplicity.

Red Skelton was not funny. Neither was Jerry Lewis. He was only funny to the French, who themselves are not funny.

A television comedy with a laugh track need not amuse. And a studio system that owned the theaters didn't need to entertain. Should it supply the advertised benefit, well and good; but here, as in Boss Tweed's New York, the bottom line was, "What are you going to do about it?"

The studios consented in 1948 to sell off their theaters. But there is no new thing under the sun; and lo, their progeny now control the production and distribution of "product."

A product is a commodity intended for sale. Its production is determined by considerations of cost and marketability. Beyond product design and packaging, beauty, even denatured as "artistic integrity," has no place in industrial thought—and design itself is constrained by cost and guesses about market strategy.

Artistic creation is absolute dedication to beauty—the artist working in Industry is, at best, and of necessity, engaged in Product Design. Conflict between him and the Executives is inevitable; the only variables are its extent and the time of its arrival.

I began my career in Hollywood at the top.

As I was a noted and successful playwright, my entry was a demotion. I was happy in the theater, in New York, knocking it out of the park; but, like all close to the Immigrant Experience, I was always looking to better capitalize my stock and my time.

The first American Jews were peddlers of needles and old clothes; their grandchildren founded the mercantile empires. My stock-in-trade was dramatic writing. It has always seemed to the uninitiated that this consisted in writing dialogue. But film writing is, actually, the construction of a plot. Films do not need dialogue. We watch foreign films, reading subtitles, and enjoy silent films with no dialogue at all. We will watch Buster Keaton all day, as we will the generally silent Hedy Lamarr.

The stage, of course, is *all* dialogue. That's how one tells *that* story; and though snappy dialogue in a film a) does not necessarily advance the plot, and b) indeed may become tiresome, ability at playwriting could buy one a ticket on the DC-3 to Los Angeles. As in my case.

So there I was, feted and petted in New York, and Bob Rafelson came to town to cast his Jack Nicholson film *The Postman Always Rings Twice* (1981).

A young friend was to audition for the part of The Girl. I asked her to tell Bob that if he didn't hire me to write the script he was nuts. She pointed out that, as they were casting, they of necessity already *had* a script.

She went to the meeting and told him anyway, and that afternoon my phone rang and Bob Rafelson said he'd seen one of my plays, he *had* no script, and would I like to write one for him?

I went to his hotel. Here are his introductory remarks:

"They're going to tell you that I threw an executive through a plate glass window. It's true."

That set the tone for forty years in Hollywood.

I did ten features as a director, the world's best job; and wrote forty or so filmscripts, half of which got made, the horror of my position as piss-boy balanced by money, spiced by wonder at the absolute inability of those who paid me to understand my scripts. No one ever liked them save the actors and the audience.


They're on the Inside, Folks, they're on the *inside*: the freaks, the frauds, the recovering virgins, the betrayed and the betrayers. Here find salacious gossip posing as information, and reminiscences that may astound and disturb and, should you love the movies, bring to your lips a wry, sad smile.

These are from the horse's mouth, the horse being the last cogent survivor of Old Hollywood. And I alone am escaped to tell thee.

*David Mamet*
*Santa Monica*

# SPEED-THE-PLOW

Life in the movie business is like the beginning
of a new love affair: it's full of surprises,
and you're constantly getting fucked.

—*Speed-the-Plow*

Washington is Hollywood for ugly people. Producing is Hollywood
for ugly people.

The actual writers, directors, and actors get into it for the fun, the
prestige, and the excitement. Some find, intermittently, some of the
above; some few find stardom, and some few make a regular living.
These last used to be the crafts-and-support folk: musicians, prop
makers, stuntfolk, model makers, armorers, dressers, and character
actors—Hollywood's mid-century equivalent of Manhattan's Lex-
ington Avenue.

These folks and their crafts are largely gone (like Lex). The parking spaces they once used are now held down by drones. The crafts
people wanted to make a living and were blessed by the ability to
do something they could sell of which they could be proud. Their
reward was not eventual but actual: they had and they held good,
satisfying jobs. But who got or gets into "producing"?

There is no day-to-day satisfaction in production, for producers,
like their kind in Washington, produce nothing. Their time, in both
cases, is spent scenting the wind and looking for an opportunity to
advance. How can one advance in an occupation that makes nothing? Through deference, betrayal, chicane, or luck. Toward what
might one advance? Power and money.

Folk music was popularized in the thirties by the musicologist Alan Lomax. He went to the Appalachians, and down south, and recorded the end-of-the-birth-of-the-blues. He was to meet Robert Johnson, who died while Lomax was in transit, and a local man suggested he meet this other fellow, Muddy Waters (with thanks to Wikipedia).

Through concerts, on the radio, and through the Smithsonian, he brought the songs to American Consciousness. And copyrighted many of them. Irving Mills produced the recordings of Duke Ellington and demanded and received co-credit for most of them.

Well, there are no new sins. Producers, like government and bank tellers, are too close to it. Their road to Damascus moment, "If I can take some of it, why not take it *all*?" Irving Mills's name on the sheet music makes me ashamed to be a Jew; and writing of Alan Lomax, ashamed to have enjoyed the Kingston Trio—their relationship to folk music as Pilates is to boxing.

Describing oneself as involved in a "relationship" is a semantic risk—the ambiguity of language, that is, lessens the ability to evaluate behavior. The terms "spouse," "partner," "mistress," "fling," "buddy"—each suggests reasonable expectations. "Producer" is a similarly ambiguous term, allowing for unfortunate latitude in behavior.

A Producer may be one who initiates, funds, or endorses a film. He may also be a colleague or assign of same. An Executive Producer is one who lends an imprimatur to the project. An Associate Producer is, as per Joe Mankiewicz, "one who would associate with a producer."

There are also those self-promoters who troll for ignorant talent, promising representation, funding, or influence. They are pimps.

None have anything to do with the actual exposure of film. The actual filmmaker must doubt and mistrust their statements and be wary of their operations, for they will never be frank, considering him, generally, a beast of burden that, curiously, has the power of speech, which speech is foolish when it is not unintelligible.

I will use the term PRODUCER in this book to refer to these.

But there is another to whom the term applies; this is the Line Producer, or UPM, Unit Production Manager. He is the General Contractor, and the filmmaker's ally and friend.

Well, it's a racket. When a racket goes legit, the thrill is gone; but the form may still be sold to those who don't quite get it. (Hefner's Playboy Clubs were whorehouses that sold everything but sex.)

Of Agents:

A friend called one the other day and was told she, the agent, was going on yet another junket-vacation. The friend asked, "When do you *work*?" And the agent said, "I'm as close as my phone."

The question, "If *what*?"

If (as was the case) the agent was just answering requests for my friend's services, why was she getting 10 percent of the take?

The truth is, if you're hot you don't need an agent; and if you're not, the agent doesn't need you.

Two CAA pitches. CAA, you will remember, was started in 1975 by Mike Ovitz and Ron Meyer. They looked the truth, above, in the face, and turned it on its head, thus: "Howzabout," they said to some very famous actors, "howzabout *we* represent you, BUT ONLY TAKE *FIVE* percent?"

They signed some few of the famous, and adjacent brothers and sisters clamored to get on the bandwagon. All the newcomers paid the Old Rate, and CAA rose to preeminence. Much of their power came through exploitation of the original stars: "I'll get you X if you take Y"; and, perhaps, "I'll give you X at a slightly reduced rate, if you take A, B, and C."

The CAA pitch of old:

"I want to be in the David Mamet business. Tell me your dreams. You want to direct more, we'll make it happen. What else? I know you write songs. You should have your own record label, we'll bring that about. And, don't you think—as we do—you should have your own Movie Company? After all, you know X, Y, and Z, and you, AND THEY, should BE IN CONTROL of output. What about your wife. What does she want? What about your dog . . . ?" No fooling.

A script of the immutability of mine when I sold carpet over the telephone. The wisdom of the boiler room, "Stick to the script, it works."

Who can resist flattery? An ancient technique of fundraisers: "How would you like your gift to be used?" Well, the gift is going to be used how and as the new owner wills.

A twice-told tale, and I hope the reader will excuse me, as this book must contain several; I trust the reader's affection—obvious from his devotion to my work sufficient to observe the repetition—will be matched by his courtesy in overlooking my senescence.

I received the above pitch from a CAA agent (Tony Krantz). He pointed out that if I wrote a half-hour pilot, I might make some real cash. How long, he said, would it take you?

"To write a half-hour pilot?" I said. "A half hour."

"For writing that pilot," he said, "I could get you two hundred thousand dollars. For one half hour's work."

"That," I said, "is four hundred grand an hour, which is sixteen million dollars a week, and eight hundred million a year, if I took two weeks off."

"If you were making that kind of money," he said, "you couldn't *afford* to take two weeks off."

Time passes, all things decay and die. I was looking for a new agent and asked my friend Ron Meyer for a recommendation.

He, that is, who was partners with Ovitz. I met him through a mutual friend when I came out to Hollywood. I was told he was a "regular guy," but how would one discover such in Hollywood?

I went to a party at his house, shot a few balls with him on his pool table. "You shoot pool," he said. "Let's shoot some pool sometime."

"Sure," I said. But the next morning he called to say he was at the pool hall near my house, and was I free? Good enough for me. An actual Studio Head (then of Paramount) who could shoot pool *and*, equally improbably, meant what he said. (And could run eighty-five balls.)

Anywaythzz (as Daffy said), I called Ron for a recommendation, and he cross-decked me to the then head of CAA, who said they'd love to have me, and he would be "Just as Close as His Phone." Having kicked me downstairs, he sent what I was free to consider the Highest of His Henchpersons out to give me the pitch.

I was looking forward to it, as one would to a beloved old movie. For was I now not Wise? I knew the charity-beggars would use my dough however they saw fit—most likely for their own salaries—and that CAA would blow smoke, and count on my cupidity to sign me up, and "put my ass on the street and bring back some money." But, wise and inured as I now was, I could be amused by (as I was, of course, immune *to*) the upcoming flattery.

But the pitch, in my case, had changed. And the triumvirate of Men in Suits explained to me that my career was over, as I'd fucked everything up; but they would take me, studio to studio, on the Perp walk, where I could apologize, and accept my now rightful place in the Applicant Pool.

"Knock knock."

"Who's there?"

"Howard."

"Howard *who*?"

"Howard the mighty fallen."

# THE LITTLE ENGINE
# AND THE FACTORY SHIP

*The Little Engine That Could* (Watty Piper, 1930) is the West's answer to the myth of Sisyphus. He, you will recall, was doomed to push a boulder perpetually up a hill, at the top of which, of course, it rolled down again. I've often wondered about his mood during the ascent, but it occurs to me it may have been even worse climbing down to retrieve the stupid rock.

But the L. Engine is the triumph of resolve over reluctance. It's Christmas Eve, and the Big Engines are, for some reason, unwilling to pull the train full of toys over the mountain to the Good Little Children.

Our Little friend knows himself to be incapable of the task, but he volunteers anyway, puffing as he pulls, his mantra "I think I can, I think I can." And he succeeds.

Because he Believed in Himself? Yup.

Greeks and the Europeans who were their philosophic like were born into their Place, and stayed there, controlled either by the Whip or by a Church which preached that God has called each man to his appointed station. It was superfluous to add, "And you'd better stay there," as there was nowhere else to go.

Until North America was opened to European immigration. And then, beginning with the western migration out of the seaboard, folk like the Little Engine could take their chances; opportunity, death, starvation, and disease bulking larger, as government and religious control diminished. And tons of millions took the bet. One hundred and change years ago, the wretched refuse had come all the way to

Hollywood. And here we still are, now in reversion to the previous Grecian paradigm.

Was ever anyone as long-suffering as Poor I, whose sole desire was to get the Toys to the Good Little Children on the Other Side of the Mountain? No.

For "mountain" we may, if we'll excuse the nicety, read "footlights"—the Good Little Children are of course our friends out there in the dark.

Previous to my Locomotive incarnation I was the Factory Ship. I'd come home from the office brooding and depressed, and my wife would say, "Oh, Dave . . . is it the 'Factory Ship' again? The Factory Ship, never stopping, never resting, never touching land, and toiling, far from notice, till the bottom rusts out and she sinks, unmourned, to the Floor of the Sea . . . ?"

"Yes," I would respond. "That's right."


Reimagined, my improved self, the engine, was first the embodiment of Descartes and then the locomotive assassin of Anna Karenina.

A two-letter man, I, both a philosopher, bringing wisdom, and a destroyer, my mission the imposition of destruction.

I won a Joke Competition in *New York* mag, decades back, by suggesting the World's Perfect Theatrical Review: "I never understood the theater until last night. Please forgive everything I've ever written. When you read this I'll be dead."

Lately, and after the demise of The Theater, my fantasy has turned to The Memorial.

Here I am, dead. And the most eloquent Speaker—have the wise planners put him first or last?—mounts the stage and says, "We shall not see his like again."

Alright, but constant recurrence to the fantasy suggested (true enough) that it was "too pat" or "off the shelf." My new favorite is a modern application of the speech uttered by the French soldier who burned Joan of Arc: "We have just killed a saint."

Who but those blessed with infinite patience and understanding would put up with the swine going pee-pee over his various Gifts to Humankind?

It is as if the Little Engine arrived, exhausted and near death, and the Good Little Children opened the boxcar doors to find not dolls and spaniel puppies but healthy, tasty vegetables. And then they killed him.

# MOTHER EARTH

Imagine engaging an artist and inquiring, as he painted, "Wait, wait, why are you putting that brushstroke *there*?" or "How will that patch of pigment increase the thing's salability?" Now you have an insight into the Producer's mind.

The afflicted painter wants to buy a ball-peen hammer and whack himself in the head till the handle breaks, but the Producer perhaps feels he is doing his job. Why? He *is* doing his job, which, after putting the project together (if indeed he's done that), is to fuck everything up.

When the lights go down you've GOT their attention. Lists of producers' logos on the screen is annoying, stupid, AND COUNTER-PRODUCTIVE. It is a vanity operation, alright, but, as the aim of the corporations should be to make money, the display of their logos, watering down the audience's attention, weakens the strength of the product. As does the endless display of the names of producers, who, in their multitude, would seem to indicate that the sole requirement for getting your name on the screen is being born.

At least back in the Studio Days they were doing whatever they did for personal gain.

Today's Executives, it seems, are ushering in an unbridled reign of Virtue. But of old, we demanded virtue only of the clergy, who, on investigation, usually proved to be as randy and sick as the rest of us.

A student of history must assume that the hegemony of the Talentless is a *result*, rather than a cause, of decomposition. One generation rises and another generation passes away, but the earth endures forever.* And Mother Earth is the great scavenger.

---

\* The Bible, a ripping good yarn.

Just as, during my lifetime, SoHo (and then Tribeca) evolved from an abandoned factory district into artist squatter housing, then into gentrification; and, catering to the gentry, into the city's eventual prime luxury shopping district; so, after the riots, begins the decay back into slums, squatter housing, and, with the death of the city, desolation.

Thus Hollywood or, more particularly, my life form, having succeeded in Hollywood and then aged out, scavenges some benefit from tell-alls, cartoons, and captions. That is my version of the faded film idol taken to shoplifting as the sole remaining possibility of maintaining public notice.

# OUT IN THE STYX

My son, Noah, age five, insisted that he was SpongeBob. His friends referred to him as Sponge, and his kindergarten teacher may have done so, too.

That Halloween we asked him if he was going to "go" as Sponge-Bob, and he said, "Why would I go as myself?"

My home and office are covered in various memorabilia. We find Judaica, and tchotchkes (objets d'art) from aviation, hunting, and the movies.* There is no theater memorabilia, which would be as viscerally abhorrent to me as would a caduceus tie clasp to a physician. Why, that is, would he want to "go" as himself?

Mr. Kipling reminds us, "We've only one virginity to lose, / And where we lost it there our hearts will be."

Pauline Kael collected her film essays in *I Lost It at the Movies*. It was the Theater that got my cherry. It was my seducer-lover, the position of debaucher reserved for a subsequent encounter.

It's said that the magic of young love is the ignorance that it can ever end; but perhaps, viewed differently, the magic continues, as the experience can be indelibly formative. The love, that is, can endure after the relationship has—necessarily—ended.

So there's Me and The Theater. But what of Me and The Movies, and the criminal dolts who came of age, not *even* in the Movies, but in The Industry?

---

* A framed yellow cloth star, JUDE; a theater-made model of a Hawker Hurricane; the 1926 *Photoplay* Magazine Medal of Honor for Best Photoplay of the Year, *Beau Geste*—the award was superseded in '28 by the Oscars.

Their reactions, over twoscore years, to craft and art (my own, most importantly) are like mine to their Industry Duplicity and ignorance: I just don't get it. *

Trolling YouTube for old films is instructive. I came across *The Enforcer*, 1951. Bogey plays a hard-hitting District Attorney. How could one have missed it? A viewing provides the answer, as it is a piece of garbage. The writers apparently had a cup of tea with a mob guy and learned that a "contract" meant a killing, and "the hit," the victim. They mentioned it scads of times, as a plot substitute. Me: Why? Wouldn't it have been more fun to *tell a story*? And my current genius line, from a forties noir: "I knew your parents before they died."

I wish I could supply you with the film's title. Apart from its magnificence the line is diagnostic. The writers thought they needed to establish that the addressee (supposed recipient of a bequest or some such thing) was newly orphaned. The line ranks with Jimmy Carter's greeting to the Poles in Polish. His inept translator, asked to have him say "I embrace you," has him up there proclaiming, "I want to fuck you."

While we're about it, a 2022 blockbuster wannabe has male stars playing cave divers, intent on rescuing some Thai boys trapped in a cave.

"Harry" shows up to round out the team. But how can they swim the boys out, through caves that daunt even our heroes? The kids could never make it. Think, think, think, and then someone says something like, "We could *drug* them! Harry's an anesthesiologist!"

Shakespeare has Richard the Second asking, "Have I no friend?"

---

* We were shooting *Heist*, Rebecca Pidgeon, my wife, playing the Bad Girl and Ricky Jay, the Utility Man. When we wrapped, the Producer continued his irrepressible depredations by selling on eBay Ricky's blue jeans and my wife's underwear.

My equivalent, of Hollywood, is, "Are *none* of you idiots paying attention . . . ?"

Well, either they or I are marching to the beat of a Different Drummer.

In which event either one or many of us must be out of step.

# TO BUILD A FIRE

A rabbi, a priest, and a zebra go into a whorehouse. The facade of this Romanesque (frequently misidentified as Beaux Arts) building brilliantly aping the best work of H. H. Richardson (1836–1886), a neighbor and sometime collaborator of Frederick Law Olmsted, creator of Central Park . . .

That's how most films are written.* They are assemblages of ideas (he wants to get the girl), and effects (a big, fat, scary monster descends from a cloud).

But every stand-up comedian knows that the extra syllable destroys the joke. These most practical of psychologists must learn the connection between their creation and the audience's attention span, or fail onstage.

The overlong setup and the delayed punch line bore the listeners, who have loaned their attention in return for the promise of amusement or surprise. The comedian not only structures the twenty-second joke but builds upon its success and *nature* to form a set that, like its component jokes, will raise, lower, and then astound expectations.

For the audience is learning, through the individual gag, what to expect from the developing set. They may, for example, appreciate a change of tempo or tone, having learned that the performer may be trusted to reward what is, after all, their faith in his ability to deliver.

---

* See "Belinda Raguesto Returns from Switzerland," from *Recessional* (2022), by this author.

Example:

Comedian: . . . and the cow was returned to its rightful owner (AUDIENCE LAUGHS).

Comedian: No, but seriously, folks, can we get serious for a moment. I'm up here "joking around," and you might think, Ha ha, but what's the *point* . . . ?

One wouldn't open a set with "No, but what is the point?," but the audience, having laughed at "the cow," has *learned* that the comedian is changing the tone merely to delight them with a surprise, AND THEY HAVE GAINED THE FAITH THAT HE WILL DO SO.

How did the comedian come by his education? Did he learn it in "Comedy School"? Should such exist, they can't teach the lesson; they can only, at best, describe or *simulate* it (like film schools) in a protected—that is, make-believe—setting.

The comedian does not read books on structure and delivery; he watches other performers, and then tries out his act onstage. And only there, and through his humiliating and thus unforgettable failures, does he develop skill.

During the westward migration myriad advice books were written on pioneering, homesteading, prospecting, and so on. But the neophyte when tired, lost, or confused was faced with imperative, baffling, and often terrifying situations which the books may have described, but did *not prepare him for.*

See Jack London's story "To Build a Fire." Here our hero, lost and shivering, manages to build that fire which alone can save him from freezing to death. He uses all his strength to gather the scant fuel, and his last match to ignite it. But he has built it under a snow-laden tree; the fire melts the snow, which falls and extinguishes it, and our hero dies.

But had he lived, there is no way on earth he would have again made the same mistake. So with the performer. The confession "I was dying up there," is as close to truth as one may get with metaphor.

The filmmaker may begin with intuition, and imitation, but his personal vision both of film and of "this" film can only develop through trial and painful error in front of an audience. Unless, of course, he doesn't care.

If he's working to please bureaucrats or their cronies, the Press and the Awards Committees, he can make his film a construction or amalgamation of elements designed to appeal to their popular prejudices: pornography, diversity, action sequences, deeply felt explications, and so on.

This is like the adolescent boy's fantasy of constructing the Perfect Mate: "The ____ of Mary; the ____ of Sue; with Betsy's ____ but Joan's intelligence."

The unschooled and virgin boy doesn't realize that any eventual mate or partner will be an actual human being, and his ignorant timidity expresses itself as a wise Epicureanism.

So it is with the dolt producers, virgin of union with an audience, employing their intelligence to fashion, like the boy, a lifeless amalgam.

# LEDA & THE SWAN,
# OR THE IMPOSSIBLE DREAM

I love old films. I have a personal (though one-way) relationship with their character actors. I think, "Man, I've got a great part for Nat Pendleton"—or Takashi Shimura, the greatest actor who ever lived. He was the star of Kurosawa's *Ikiru*, and the head samurai (the Yul Brynner role) in *Seven Samurai*.

Kurosawa's rep company was also graced by Seiji Miyaguchi. In *Seven Samurai* he played the great swordsman (James Coburn in *The Magnificent Seven*). Miyaguchi copped to being 5'3", which means he was probably 5'2". I mention it because the camera sees only what you instruct it to see. Not only is a person's height irrelevant, so is his behavior prior to "action." The audience starts looking when one turns the camera on.

But we are curious. As we are about all heroes more nuanced than "a handsome prince" or "a beautiful maiden," at bedtime. Celebrity inflames our hunger for gossip. The supermarket mag and Roman myths are both gossip about the gods. Our thirst for their modern equivalent is *unslakable*—else most contemporary media would curl up and die.

Why? We aren't made insomniac by our online investigation of the private lives of classical musicians or dentists. But we *see* celebrities writ large, and we understand them as demigods, which is to say as improved versions of ourselves. How strong is our need for unity with those Immortals? It can never be assuaged.

And what is it we want to know?

A friend, a sexual profligate, told me of a similar irresolvable longing. "The problem with sex with two women," he said, "is that when you're watching, all you want to do is participate, and when you're doing it, all you want to do is watch."*

Here his desire for some greater communion has doomed him to perpetual disappointment. As with King Kong and Fay Wray: the King is doomed not only to the agony of an unconsummatable love but to the denial of all unsexual intercourse, courting or flirting, e.g., "What's your major . . . ?" And we are doomed to disappointment of a consummation with Movie Stars; it's *just* not taking place.

Our interest persists, inflamed by their remove. When it wanes they are no longer Fantasy Boffo and we graze in celebrity pastures new. Prior to that, you and I want to know all about them.

Online sites for the inquisitive have long featured lists of the stars' amours. Our interest here is masochistic; while we enjoy the sexual gossip, it comes with the knowledge that they are cheating on us. For what in the world are they, up there on the screen, but sexual objects; and like the Priests of Ancient Israel, they must have no defect.

Stars, being actually human, do have defects, but the camera can frame them out. Hair, makeup, and lights skew the image just as infatuation and lust do in Real Life. So the camera sees with the eyes of love. How terrible, then, to find that this busload of critters named names to the FBI, or that that carload murdered their wives.

During courtship we do not want our beloved revealed as human. The human mind and physiology will flood us with endorphins sufficient to overlook both solecisms of behavior and the odd scrap of lettuce in the teeth. The appearance of the stars, their speech, and their behavior are all prepared for us. But we *cannot* get close enough to them. For any possible proximity destroys the illusion.

Michael Caine and Sean Connery are accepted as gods among the Mountain folk in *The Man Who Would Be King*. Sean wants to wed a local beauty. She resists, as congress with a god would mean her

---

* With the addition of Just One Extra Woman they could have played whist.

instant death. He tries to kiss her, and she bites him. The Tibetans see blood and realize Sean is not a god, and they kill him.

Sean himself was a lovely man. His first words to me (on *The Untouchables*), "I never made a penny off of Bond."[*]

And I spent an evening at Sue Mengers's with Michael Caine, who was kind enough to respond to my request for inside info about Nigel Green. The odd, tough character actor played the Colour Sergeant in Caine's first big film, *Zulu*, and the bad guy in *The Ipcress File*. Michael told me Nigel had committed suicide, and I was sad for his trouble, for the loss to film, *and* that I would then never have the chance to work with him. But as he had made his films when I was still in high school—the collaboration never would have been possible. My longing was no less real for all that my recognition of it revealed its impossibility.

Just like our wish for congress with Movie Stars—for what else are they selling? Didn't Rita Hayworth inform us, "They go to bed with Gilda, but they wake up with Rita."

I fell in love with Myrna Loy on our afternoon together in 1980. I was married, and thirty-two, she was seventy-five, and I will flatter myself that the feeling may have been shared. But we recall Shakespeare's "The course of true love never did run smooth; / But, either it was different in blood— / . . . Or else misgraffed in respect of years—"

I also fell in love, of course, with Audrey Hepburn, and I think I could have made her happy.

---

[*] I beg pardon, for I've written this story before; but for the uninitiated, and as a public service, here's what you should know about Sean: He was in Majorca, we were speaking on the phone about something or other. I'd just gotten off the phone with my sister, who was in the midst of a marital catastrophe. I told her I'd have to ring off, as I had a business call with Sean. She said, "Lucky you," and "Please tell him I adore his work." I called Sean and apologized for my unpunctuality. I explained that I was comforting my sister, and that I had promised to tell him that she adored his work. He asked for her number and, after our call, rang her up in Ohio and chatted for half an hour.

# EARLY FILMS

In our period of racial aphasia, The Movies, as always, are first among Equals in fear of The Mob—my marvelous art form, but lickspittle racket.

Now, when Putting Up Signs is considered a brave act of conscience, we find an entire half of the populace adopting the movies' charade, of valor by proxy—this the endgame of their relationship with an industry that once sold popcorn.

Lena Horne was not permitted to play an octoroon in *Pinky* because she was Black. Natalie Wood was shoveled into every role for a woman of color because her skin "took" the Hershey's Syrup well. Klaus Kinski* played the head of an Israeli Mossad unit in *The Little Drummer Girl*, Charlie Chan was played by a Swede, Mr. Moto by a Hungarian Jew; and the most memorable Nazi portrayals were those of Conrad Veidt, a Jew.

The Indians were played by Woody Strode, an African American, and Anthony Quinn and Ricardo Montalban, both Mexicans; while the Mexicans were played by Wallace Beery (*Viva Villa!*), Brando (*Viva Zapata!*), and Jack Palance (*The Professionals*).

Duncan Renaldo, the Cisco Kid, was born Vasile Dumitru Cugheanos, in Romania. Robert Donat played a half-Chinese, half-white man in *The Inn of the Sixth Happiness*, and Mickey Rooney (!) a Japanese photographer in *Breakfast at Tiffany's*; Dame Judith

---

* Who served in the German Wehrmacht during World War II.

Anderson was the Native American matriarch in *A Man Called Horse*.

It was crazy, disrespectful, and agonizing to members of the slighted groups, but at least it was recognizable as a human reaction: it was prejudice. The tough-guy Jews who were the business, the hard-drinking, hard-whoring gamblers and thugs, bit their nails over "offending" majority Americans. Now the feared objects are not the mass but the minorities. This, though affording a demonic balance, makes, otherwise, as much sense as casting Paul Muni as Benito Juárez. It is now, as it was then, a sop to a perceived audience, which would not tolerate a white girl being kissed by Sidney Poitier but flocked to see Fay Wray being raped by a gorilla.

How odd, our human obsession with The Other. This is the engine of pornography, rendering thrilling the commonplace (everyone's either got an innie or an outie) by showing it on-screen. The assertion of novelty renders it noteworthy, while the actually novel, casting a Jew as a Jew, was shunned as "too."

And many of the Space Alien roles were assigned to The Other in order to keep the films Pure. See Ricardo Montalban as Khan in the *Star Trek* films, my landsman Leonard Nimoy as Spock, James Earl Jones as the voice of Darth Vader, and Charles Middleton (born Chaim Mirsky, Lodz, 1892)* as Flash Gordon's nemesis, Ming the Merciless.†

See also Broadway's 1979 *The Elephant Man*, Bernard Pomerance's play starring Philip Anglim as John Merrick, a horribly

---

\* A complete fabrication.—*Ed.*

† In Atlanta, in 1913, a young factory girl was raped and murdered. Her supervisor, Leo Frank, was accused, and convicted in spite of his obvious innocence and an alibi. He was dragged from prison and lynched by a mob yelling, "Death to the Jew." The case was dramatized in the 1937 film *They Won't Forget*. Here, however, the film's citizens framed and killed him because he was a "damned Yankee."

The 1947 film *Crossfire* is a film noir based on the novel *The Brick Foxhole*. In the book, drunken GIs on leave are invited to a party and murder the host because he is gay. In the film, they kill him because he is a Jew. Call me crazy.

deformed Victorian man working as a sideshow freak, who is be-friended and discovered to have a deep soul and a fine mind. The Broadway audience enjoyed the play and applauded themselves for accepting his deformity—easy to do, as Anglim was a beautiful young man (dressed, intermittently, in a loincloth) whose deformity consisted in his arranging himself into a pretzel.

"Illness" dramas have been replaced by "Diversity" porn. Both violate Aristotle's dictum that the Hero's progression must devolve from his *choice*, and never from his *condition*.

Well, what doesn't go bad? The food with the longest shelf life is the least edible; and, vice versa, the most succulent food is that fresh from the garden—the garden here, perhaps, the interaction of inspired humans (enthused by love, or greed) and novelty.

For who would have stooped to pick up the unnoticed novelty (the cinematograph, or the Hula-Hoop) but those with vision. The vision might be of wealth, or of adventure, but it could only occur—the possibility of the overlooked—to the hungry and enthused. The rich man won't stoop in the street to pick up a dime. The billion-aire's children wouldn't pick up a dollar. (Why would they be on the street?)

Victorian fantasy had the young man schlepping to Paris to dis-cover himself, as today's blighted youth crowds into film school. Both are the equivalent of the Charles Atlas comic book courses in Physical Culture: "I was a 97-pound weakling, and the bully at the beach kicked sand in my face, but *now* . . ."

The Paris-bound, like the film school grads, were paid (then, by Mom and Dad; now, it seems, by Mom and Dad in our capacity as the Tax Base) to keep themselves out of the workforce.

It was long said that California needed illegal immigrants, as Americans would not do stoop labor. Now, the only folks working in the Golden State are the progeny of those stoop laborers; and, at the outside, fifty years at most, we Anglos will be mowing *their* lawns. How could it be otherwise? They're the only group paying attention.

Meanwhile, as the Movie Industry ennobles this or that individ-ual on the basis of an Acknowledged Group *complaint*, the ability of the individual to produce, improve, or indeed comprehend the basic activity is considered moot.

It is the same idiocy that cast Natalie Wood as the Puerto Rican girl named Maria. And it is only an inbred delicacy that prohibits me from suggesting that the film biz is expiring like Miss Wood, drowned by our own mink coat.

# HATS AND SHOES

The studios' costumes (in the black-and-white days) were magnificent. The industry supported a population of hundreds of (predominantly Italian) tailors. All of the male stars' suits were made-to-order by masters. I don't know where or if one could achieve that quality today.

Not only were the suits cut perfectly—that is, to accentuate the star's best features—but the fabrics were chosen for their ability to catch the light.

Female stars, each of whom had her favorite designer, were appreciated not only for their acting ability but for their presentation of a fashion show.

Some would change outfits fifteen times in a film. (Kay Francis was followed by women fans who came to see what she was going to wear.) And women were, then, not only the largest percentage of moviegoers but noted as tiebreakers in spousal discussions of which movie to watch.

A large part of the fashion interest and curiosity was The Hat.

These were designed and employed, onstage and off-, to call attention to the face, accentuating, masking, suggesting, or teasing through the shape, the tilt, the adornment, and the veil. The glance was drawn to the hat, and the attention stayed on the face.

The aspect ratio (height to width) of the screen was then 1:1.33, perfect for a close-up, and approximated today on iPhones as Portrait mode.

The close-up sold the face. The hat and clothes were designed with that intent. Frills, heavy necklaces, busyness around the shoulders and throat, distracted from the star's face, which, finally, was what the studios were selling. The wise director used the hat just as the actresses and their sisters did, to command the eye. ("The hand is quicker than the eye" is an inaccurate description of close-up magic. The hand is *not* quicker than the eye. Manipulation consists in forcing the viewer to look where you need him to look.)

Men were easier to clothe, as the suit coat or sport coat naturally draws the eye to the face—the V of the jacket, the collar points, and the tie all drawing the eye up, as did Brando's leather jacket, and Bogey's turned-up-collared trench coat.

The women's hats made it challenging to light the face, so the director and the Director of Photography (DP) had to give it some thought. The artists among them realized that this offered not constraint but possibility. (See Rembrandt, a painter.)

The hat-wearing star *needed* to be lit from below or from the side. (As Joe Sternberg did with Dietrich.)

Most films today, and all comedies, drench the screen with light, devoted not to the *creation* but to the *recording* of a story. It's not only boring but confusing, as, if everything is lit evenly, the audience is not aided in their quest for pertinent information.

How important is the distinction between thoughtful (let alone artistic) and cover-the-earth lighting? See Sternberg's *Dishonored*, 1931.

Here Sternberg casts Dietrich as the most glamorous spy of World War I. She is sent, undercover, to Russia. Her cover is the bovine Slavey, and there she is, up on a ladder, all dirndled out, and unrecognizable. Even knowing she is Dietrich, we don't recognize her. The makeup helped the disguise, which was achieved, more importantly, by the lighting. He didn't *light* her as Dietrich.

\*  \*  \*

Men stopped wearing hats in 1959, when John Kennedy showed up at a ball game bareheaded. The next morning the men's Hat Industry was dead.

Women in my mother's time wore hats to go Downtown Shopping. And they smoked. The hats and the cigarettes drew attention to the face—one could at any moment adjust, remove, or replace the hat or the veil, or take another puff and exhale the smoke, wreathing the face, and so on . . .

Today's women perform the same instruction to the viewer by tossing their hair, or indeed by turning away, the motion drawing the eye of its intended recipient.

This, like arranging the hair, raised the breast in an immemorial bid for male attention—not a strategy but a survival mechanism.

Today they do not wear hats. The interest, care, money, and imagination once devoted to them have gone elsewhere—into shoes. My wife refers to money as "shoe coupons."

A luxury shoe store in my neighborhood has been smashed-and-grabbed several times in the last three years—the purloined shoes can be sold on the internet, price cut, no questions asked, resembling, in this, the historical use of the movies as a laundromat for money. It comes in with no questions asked (dirty), it goes out, as movie revenue, clean as a hound's tooth.

I asked my wife why the interest in shoes. Victorian men admired a woman's ankles, as, apart from the face, they were the sole part of the anatomy not disguised in drapery. But, I said, today's men look at neither feet nor shoes. "Women do," she said. Ah.


I did a film with a fly-by-night producer who'd started as a dry cleaner.

He was an immigrant, moved to Hollywood. He noticed that the rich folk here would pay much more than the going rate for their cleaning, as they didn't *know* what the cost of their cleaning was—they would dispatch their housekeeper or "Household Manager" to pick up the cleaning, and no one ever saw, let alone questioned, the bills. He started cleaning for the movies.

He saw that dry cleaning was a small part of the Costumes Budget, which was a small part of the whole, so began brutally raising his prices, and was thrilled to find that nobody noticed. Hmm, he thought, or words of that sort, I have to look *into* this movie business; and he did.

He found, like our beloved Mafia of old, that *every* aspect of a business could be exploited.

The Mafia didn't have to own the business they strong-armed, they just had to demand that the proprietor buy their beer, food, linens, and garbage collection, and hire employees from Mafia-controlled unions.

Those shook down couldn't squawk. (To whom, when the Mafia owned the cops?) And the movie folk couldn't squawk to the dry cleaner, as they weren't paying attention. So he branched out into catering, car rental, costume rental, and other constituent film services.

As he got deeper and deeper into the thing, chuckling at the criminal carelessness of the studios, he realized that if these idiots could succeed at the racket, what could *he* not do?

And so he became a movie producer.

Now the vast horizon of the New Day opened to him, as did the continent before Lewis and Clark.

Not only could he scam on *every department* in the making of a film—costumes, equipment rental, transportation, catering, housing—but he could milk the investors, financing a supposedly five-million-dollar film for four, by the simple provision of a second set of books.

He adopted the now standard ruse of approaching the director just before principal photography, confessing the film underfunded, and requesting (demanding) that the director waive his fee. (Every time.) And he added his own real, if inflated and actually fictional, Production Costs to the budget.

One of his henchmen, in a city some five hundred miles away, was jotted down for private jet fare, every week, back and forth to the set. The dull enormity was enlivened by the discovery that the so-called producer never in fact even left home. There was no jet—the school-days lessons of dry cleaning once again paid: no one was watching the books.

The studios did it differently. They were minting money, and they in-housed the various departments, keeping costs legitimately low through volume. But they scammed on the other end. They hid income from profit participants, even on huge moneymakers—they charged back "embedded" costs from failed films of yore they had made.

Film Insiders for years enjoyed a scam of investment in a "package" of films, the profits skimmed from the top, and tax losses taken against the losers.*

Another producer stole my contingency.

Independent films are made with a budget, an insurance policy (what happens if someone breaks an ankle?), and a contingency fund.

The contingency fund is Mama's Bank Account. It's there for a rainy day—a scene that needs to be reshot, too many days of rain, and various everyday occurrences. Most or all independent films come up short or close to it, as they're being made fast and cheap. So the contingency is a cushion.

On this film of mine, there was no money budgeted for post-production—editing, sound, effects, processing, titles, music: one-third of the time and effort spent on a film.

*No* money budgeted. But, it was explained to me before I began, I could use the unspent contingency. It was up to me. If I, the director, was careful in principal photography, I'd have the cash to finish the film. Take it or leave it.

It was a logical, if harsh, challenge. I told them I could bring the film in at X; and if I was so all-fired sure of myself, I could go ahead, and bet on myself. I did.

---

* They also scammed, then as now, with the float, taking all income immediately but paying out, if forced, after all possible delay, and keeping the interest.

I wrapped the film on schedule and on budget. And the contingency was gone.

G. Oh. En. Eee.

We were calling from the editing room to get a messenger, as FedEx had canceled our account for nonpayment. The money was *gone*.

Where, I asked my then colleague (one of the producers), *was* the contingency? "What are you talking about?" he explained.

It had joined the killer of Ron and Nicole.

We finished the film—due largely to the efforts of Barbara Tulliver, its editor. We went to the premiere, Barbara and I, wearing T-shirts reading LOSE ONE MILLION DOLLARS FROM YOUR CONTINGENCY: ASK ME HOW!

The film's producer—he who began the project as my friend and ended it in cahoots with another bottom-feeder he'd brought on (presumably his new guru)—threw a fit. "What did you *mean*," he asked, "impugning my honor?"

I still don't know how we finished the film.

Now film budgets are diverted not only to the sustenance of scads of lemmings called Producers but to various set harpies, political commissars, COVID annoyers, and other attack-puritans, sustained by an age and industry that has forgotten the phrase "Mind your own business."

In Ted Morgan's biography of Maugham, we find The Master searching for the accurate cockney term for one of his characters. He asks a Cockney: If you wanted someone to go away, would you say, "Cop it," or "Git out of it . . . ?" "You mean," the fellow said, "if I wanted to tell someone to fuck off . . . ?"

In the age of Netflix, Apple, et al., the opportunities for theft are both lessened and unnecessary. The hegemons can charge whatever they want to a captive audience, and pay whatever they want to a captive workforce.

In Communist Russia this resulted, in painting, in Socialist Realism; and, in film, to *Me and My Tractor*. The reader will, of course, draw whatever parallels he finds amusing.

But to return to hats and shoes.

The particularities change, but the form persists. Once a co-dependent populace staged wet T-shirt contests for middle-aged men. These were called the high school car wash.

Today in Los Angeles the teenage girls walk about virtually naked, and the males, rather than getting a pass for ogling the good clean fun, are terrified of even inadvertent gawking.

But the urge is innate—males are physiologically drawn to admire beauty and are aroused by the visual. (Or else the porn mega-industry is very mistaken indeed and must be operating at a loss.)

Women wore hats, certainly, to distinguish themselves from other women, with whom they were in competition—for what? For Males, the hat itself operating as does the unique appendage of the lantern fish.

The impulse persists—to "monetize," as it were, the body, or, better, to use its adornment for a social purpose. But the shoes, though they support the women in competition with her kind, do not attract men, and are not intended to.

And the movies, to arrive at a perhaps clumsy but nonetheless accurate end, today are made and advertised not to excite the natural thirst for adventure and novelty but to satisfy the human desire for conformity. They are no longer, like the Hat of old, in the service of Eros.

# GOSSIP

I don't read the books friends send me. I will give them a sentence or two, out of respect; but, my suspicions confirmed, I put them aside. Most of them are accompanied by the friend's opinion that the subject should interest me. But I discard them not because of their subjects but because of the writing.

I'll read the instructions for a hammer, if well written; and until the plague of social conformity, I never found a subject that didn't interest me. Inequity, Gender Politics, Feminism, and like doctrines are like modern art: a first glance is sufficient. There's no information to be gained from an in-depth study.

Shel Silverstein hipped me onto various treasures, endorsed not because of subject but because of their beauty.

He delighted to share with the unaccountably deprived. "What," for example, "do you mean you've never heard of Bolitho?" He thought *Twelve Against the Gods* was the most magnificent of books, and so do I. And I, in my ignorance, had never heard of the Victorian writer Ernest Bramah, and his pee-one's-pants funniest of accounts of Kai Lung, Bramah's Chinese Storyteller: "The elder and less attractive of the maidens fled, uttering loud and continuous cries of apprehension in order to conceal the direction of her flight."

Shel had read everything in the world. Like my friend the great Ricky Jay, on whom more later, he was a high school dropout.

Anouk Aimée (born Nicole Françoise Florence Dreyfus) was the loveliest woman of her age, and one of the great (uncredited) Jewish

Beauties. In Lelouch's 1960 Chocolate Box love story *Un Homme et une Femme*, she describes her young son's school report to Jean-Louis Trintignant, her lover (*"Intelligent, mais paresseux"*): intelligent, but lazy; proving the universality of the canard.

They said it of me, and likely of you; and after they'd said it Just Enough, Shel and Ricky dropped out of school.

I heard it again, at dinner one night, a school's report of a friend's kid. So, like *Star Wars* and the Vampire, apparently it just won't die. But what can it mean, other than that the teacher is incompetent?

As he recognizes intelligence, isn't he being paid to *interest* the student in it? He is.

It is a confession framed as an indictment, *sic*, "the kid should be intelligent enough to see that I am doing a fine job." But in effect, he is sufficiently intelligent to perceive the reverse. His laziness might be a visceral inability to stand boredom. How might this intelligent inability be turned into education? By a teacher whose interest in his subject communicated itself to his charges.

Shel's or Ricky's "Wait, you've never heard of . . . ?" sent me to the bookstore every time.

Likewise with movies.

Scott Rudin produced a bunch of wonderful films (*No Country for Old Men, The Addams Family, School of Rock*, and thirty more). Being a producer, he is my enemy. But as a snakebit film buff, he is my friend; we could sit for hours over what long ago had been lunch, trading movie lore and trivia. It seems he knows every film ever made. I could never stump him. /

And now our orbits have diverged; he, still, wherever he is, and myself, now the Hermit of Santa Monica, shunning a world that has moved on, and to which his name is as the mention of Herodotus to illiterate youth.

From *Squirrels* (Mamet, 1973), "Ah, Time, Time, Time, you old pee-pee head." The character is The Cleaning Lady (first played by Linda Kimbrough), the real brains of a Writers Room comprised of an ancient Hack (me), and a young Postulant (similarly).

She continues, "Though it is, of course, odd to speak of Time as being Old." (Pause) "You *young* pee-pee head . . . ?"

As racing drivers discuss compression-ratios, and lawyers their new watch, we buffs get high on arcana. "Hey, wait a second," one might say after the second pot of coffee: "Did you know that Francis Lederer, the love-interest for Louise Brooks in *Pandora's Box* (1929 Pabst classic femme fatale silent, in which Louise wore and created her signature Flapper Bob), made a fortune buying up The Valley . . . ?"

"Did you see John Qualen (he who played the Swedish Immigrant in ninety films, unforgettable as the dust bowl farmer, confronting the sheriffs in *The Grapes of Wrath*: 'Doesn't anyone know what a *shotgun* is . . . ?'), as an extra in *The Last Command*?" (Sternberg's silent 1928 film of a Russian field marshal reduced to playing bits in Hollywood.) "Yes," one would respond, "*and*, who plays the film dir—" Response, "Yes, yes, yes, Bill Powell; and did you know that he and Jean Harlow . . ." "Yes, yes, and did you know that she did *not* die of a Christian Science Mother who refused to have her operated on, but . . ." And so on, addictive and inexhaustible.

Those things shared might be described as *culture*, that is, the dedication, out of love or conviction, to a common endeavor, which endeavor might be identified by its title, but accurately understood only through its shared myths.

There's George Sanders, an extra, asleep in a jeep in *I Was a Male War Bride*; there's Cary Grant, in drag, which is the joke within the joke of Tony Curtis playing him in *Some Like It Hot*; and did you remark that it was always Cary who was the Pursued in his sex comedies? And how could Hedy Lamarr have come to such a sad end? Likewise her legion of Thespian Sisters; and Karen Morley blacklisted, and Pert Kelton bounced from her spot as the original Alice Kramden in *The Honeymooners* because her husband had been blacklisted; and I know a guy who knows a woman who was in the FBI back then, and here's who *she* said actually killed Marilyn . . . And what do you make of all these post-facto exposés by this or that pimp slandering those beyond legal redress . . . ?

So many films are lost. At least two-thirds of all movies made are gone, withered on the acetate stock or pulped in World War II for the nitrates to make gunpowder.

Trivia is gossip without malice.

I introduced myself to Sylvia Sidney in the lobby of the Chateau Marmont in 1980. The Chateau was the studios' barracks for Englishmen and New York writers whoring around Hollywood. It was an atrocious fleabag. Nothing worked, the shower handles and the doorknobs came off in the hand, it was filthy.

Miss Sidney was, most apparently, waiting to meet a director who might have a job for her. Other waiting womenfolk were mostly the call girls, their lower-rent sisters prowling the sidewalk across Sunset.

Two blocks down Sunset was Schwab's Pharmacy, apocryphal site of Lana Turner's discovery. Next door to the Chateau was the Imperial Gardens, which had been Preston Sturges's restaurant, wherein he went broke and was shepherded from failure and poverty by Jimmy Conlin, who played the bug-eyed convict in *Sullivan's Travels* and was a comic staple of Sturges's troupe.

Sylvia was, at one point, married to Luther Adler, of the great Yiddish theater clan. He was a Broadway star and a featured player in the movies. His sister Stella, a noted teacher, had been married to Harold Clurman, the Broadway director dear to me because of this exchange: "Mr. Clurman, a director has such responsibilities, what do you do when you've done something unforgivable?"

Harold: "Forgive yourself."

Contemporary swine have trotted out the old anti-Semitic canards: that the Jews control this or that. If only. Further, the indictment doesn't specify in what ways Jews exercise this supposed control, and how it injures the ranters who, universally, seem to have done right well in Show Biz *whoever* controls it; and, should this prove to be "the Jews," perhaps thanks are more appropriate than invective.

Well, the Boys controlled boxing, betting, Vegas, and so on. But one never heard the winner complain; and the cries of the losers were curiously only directed against the Fates, the Cards, or the Spread, Italians being exempt.

Q. Do/did the Jews control Hollywood?

A. Kiss my ass.[*]

The call for equity is a demand for reward without achievement; and the Studios that heed it are, consequently, turning out garbage.

But there was Sylvia Sidney, probably seventy years old, with her svelte body and the cat-face so beloved of male movie fans.

I introduced myself and she looked right past me or through me and I saw that her problems, in that lobby, were greater than mine; and that, although I had a Theatrical Pedigree, she, quite rightly, didn't give a damn.

I also burbled over Robert Mitchum one year at Cannes, which burg was probably undergoing a booze shortage since his arrival. But I have been drunk myself.

---

[*] We Jews, though very active in Hollywood, do nothing to promote either Judaism or our co-religionaries. We would sooner be caught dead, as, to our minds, nothing would more easily identify us as despicable than group solidarity. We have a two-thousand-year-long horror of being singled out. But with the exception of mass extermination (Europe, 1940–45), we understood that our enemies could only kill *some* of us. Whom would they target? Those who were conspicuous and disavowed by their more powerful brethren.

Gays, Lesbians, Blacks, and Hispanics take pride in promoting their like. But we Jews will advance the visible of our kind only after a sort of baptism. Ira Grossel becomes Jeff Chandler; Mikhail Igor Peschkowsky, Mike Nichols.

A rare example of interfaith philo-Semitism:

Joe Mantegna was for years the voice of Mercedes-Benz.

I asked him, "Joe, do they treat you well?"

"You bet, Dave."

"Give you a new car every year?"

"Top-of-the-line."

"Joe, do you get the leather upholstery?"

"Of course."

"Joe," I said, "how can you drive a car, knowing the seats may be made from the skin of my grandfather?"

"Dave," he said, "they give me the car, I look over every inch of that leather; and if I see THEM LITTLE FUCKING NUMBERS . . ."

As part of the Jewish cabal of Broadway-Acting Studios and Hollywood, I was friendly with Herbert Berghof* and Uta Hagen—HB Studio. Stella Adler, HB, the Neighborhood Playhouse, and the Actors Studio were all Jewish Pushcarts. That is, like Donald Hall's great kids' book *Ox-Cart Man*, the immigrant Jew sold everything on his cart, then sold the cart, then sold the ox.

The acting studios had the Ashkenazi flavor of Talmud Study, psychoanalysis, and Marxism, mixed to taste and reconstituted as Emotional Memory and confession.

It was a lot of blather, but I do not indict the teachers' sincerity—they were trying to impart a vision. Unfortunately, the vision's actual name was Talent, and it cannot be approached through doctrine masquerading as technique.

After the Golden Age and World War II, Hollywood's stars came not from the streets, diners, and high schools of this great land but from the New York Stage, and the New York studios with which they were intertwined. Notable among the Jewish schools (identified here as such for the first time) was Juilliard.

Juilliard was the upscale (read: supposedly non-Jewish) École Polytechnique of Acting Schools. It taught voice, diction, singing, dance, posture, and the odd acting class. It was the Oxbridge to the others' Storefront Shul versions of instruction. Its vision was that of John Houseman, its director. He'd been the producer of Orson Welles's Mercury Theatre, *Citizen Kane*, *On Dangerous Ground*, *The Blue Dahlia*, and other great films. He was born Jacques Haussmann, in Bucharest, Romania, but always appeared and sounded like a British gentleman (read: goy).

I knew him well.

---

* Herbert grew up in Vienna. He told me that when the '31 film of *An American Tragedy* opened, he and his friends watched every showing through the week, entranced by Sylvia Sidney's XCU smile. She played the discarded factory girl, the part played by Shelley Winters, another of my people, in George Stevens's masterpiece retelling, *A Place in the Sun*, 1951.

Reported previously: I'm asleep in Chicago in 1976. Five a.m., the phone rings, I answer it.

Me: "Hello . . . ?"

John (English Aristo voice): "Mamet?"

Me: "Hello, John."

John: "Mamet, I have a confession to make."

Me: "Alright."

John: "I'm queer." (Long pause.) "For your writing."

He was great friends with Norman Lloyd, of the Mercury Theatre and Hitchcock's films (the title role in *Saboteur*).

Norman died in 2021, at 106. He lived around the corner; I got to hear many of his stories. He was in the cast of Welles's 1938 *War of the Worlds* radio broadcast and was arrested and hauled off to jail with the cast and crew—those in the studio were among the sole Americans unaware the Martians had landed. "We were puzzled," he said.

John was staying at Norman's house some years back. He went out in his bathrobe and slippers to pick up the paper. He bent over, revealing his bare behind.

Norman: John, you shouldn't do that, somebody driving home drunk might mistake it for the Holland Tunnel and drive up your ass.

John was married to the gorgeous Zita Johann, who was the love interest of Boris Karloff in *The Mummy*, the 1932 film. She was Jewish too, what are you going to do about it?

# THE FORM PERSISTS

Even, and perhaps especially, in revolutionary upheavals we see that the form persists.

The revolutionists can change the slogans and supplant those currently in power with their own. They will call this justice, but it's only switching the racing colors on the jockeys.

The fascists and the Communists banished Religion, but both the Hammer and Sickle and the swastika are crosses; and Lenin took much of his strategy from the Jesuits.

The white hegemony in a century of pictures has been replaced by a Black hegemony*—each is a struggle for power over competitors and its imposition on a (perceived) audience.

1940s: "Of course there are no Black Stars, what *are* you, a _#$%^& Lover . . . ?"

2022: "Of course we are only casting People of Color, what *are* you, a Racist?"

This is close to the mechanics of the porn industry, casting the Male Lead based on the size of the fellow's penis (his performance is actually irrelevant, as the film can be *cut*).

As films approach near and nearer to outright pornography, the current mechanism of control becomes clearer. A question: Is it a "good idea" to make *Wuthering Heights* with a mixed-race cast? Yes? No? How about a biography of Harry Truman, with the lead portrayed by an Asian woman? If that seems absurd, perhaps the entire mechanism might stand some scrutiny.

---

* A market strategy engineered by the white hegemony.

Are current executives skewing the casting process "in good faith"? When did they ever do anything in good faith?

In the old days, Directors came up through the ranks, and got their jobs, in the main, because they became skilled at doing what they loved.

Those in the Italian suits might condescend to spend a quarter hour on the set, trying to stay awake and smiling. But we actual moviemakers loved it.

Mike Nichols had a framed *New Yorker* cartoon in his living room. Two circus seals, one saying to the other, "Of course, what I'd *really* like to do is direct."

Where did the directors come from? Many of the greats were originally actors. And many wrote and directed the films that they starred in. I cite the Three Originals, Harold Lloyd, Charlie Chaplin, and, the greatest of the greats, Buster Keaton. And many of their progeny began as actors and went on to direct: Vittorio De Sica, Jean Renoir, Mel Brooks, Woody Allen; and Jules Dassin and Barbara Loden.

Jules was blacklisted by McCarthy and went to France. He had no money and didn't speak the lingo, but he'd directed *Night and the City*, *Brute Force*, and *The Naked City*, three of the great tough-guy films. He found a little cash and made the best of heist films, *Rififi*.

The fellow cast as the Italian Safecracker in *Rififi* got sick, and Jules stepped in to play his part.

There were always great women directors. What better documentarian than Leni Riefenstahl? (All that to one side.) We had our Dorothy Arzner, turning a significant contribution to Gay Film, with Kate Hepburn as the aviator Christopher Strong.

And our gallant Soviet ally had the works of Larisa Shepitko, than whom no better director ever lived (*The Ascent*, *Letter Never Sent*).

Barbara Loden (1932–1980) was a fine actress. (See her in *Wild River* or *Splendor in the Grass*.) She was married to Elia Kazan.

She wrote, directed, and starred in *Wanda* (1970), as good and odd a crime drama as it's possible to make. It was said that Kazan gave her a hard time about the film, and I don't doubt it, as she was the better director.

She had, and he did not, that which our Teutonic Friends call *Fingerspitzengefühl*, feeling in one's fingers. (See the films of Paul Thomas Anderson.)

In a Kazan film one could admire this or that "touch," but one never responds that way to a film of Paul's, as one is actually otherwise occupied, engrossed in the entertainment.

Kazan was successful, inter alia, as a conversationalist, for did he not share the names of all his friends with the House Un-American Activities Committee?

And today, Show Biz trembles under the constant threat of denunciation.

As with the cross and the swastika, the situation continues, the new practitioners merely changing their name tags. The impulse to obey, to go along in order to get along, not to make waves, and, finally, to escape censure or pain, persists, it being a cornerstone of human nature.

For what sin is committed other than for a Good Cause? The cause may be "peace," or The Atmosphere, or Equity, or (most usually) "because I want it and I'm worth it" (whatever the object of desire). Who ever says, "I'm doing this because it's a bad idea"?


Dino De Laurentiis and Ridley Scott one summer came to Martha's Vineyard to convince me to write the script for *Hannibal*.

I asked Dino about his longtime colleague De Sica. He said De Sica was a degenerate gambler who'd borrow money from him in the casino, run off to lose it, and return to mortgage his next two or three films in return for more. (We can see De Sica in his *Gold of Naples* playing an addicted gambler deprived of funds, across the kitchen table from a ten-year-old boy, gambling for matches.)

I wrote the *Hannibal* script, and, right on time, they hated it. They fired me and hired Steve Zaillian to write a new one.

He called me before the film was released, and said that, in justice, I should take the sole screen credit, as, in justice, it was my script on which Scott relied. (Greeks bearing gifts.)

That's right. I went to the premiere, and there was my name in first position, but where was my script? They'd shot what I assume was Zaillian's script, which was a pile of shit, as was the film; and I have to give Zaillian credit for his perfidy, as he gave credit to me for the film.

My first impression of Movies, being in, came at the meet and greet for *Postman*. Chateau Marmont, 1980: in attendance, Jack Nicholson, Jessica Lange, Bob Rafelson, and me.

Jessica had just returned from making *King Kong*. She treated us to her rendition of the film's producer, Dino De Laurentiis.

"Whenn-a dan new Kong die, *evvraboddy* gonna cry."

Jessie played Frances Farmer in that biopic.

This is an irrefutable sign of decay, songs about songwriters, films about stars; what can it mean other than an announcement that the Great Days Are Gone, and the attempt to monetize their residue?

Jessie was wonderful in *Frances*, as she is in everything; but biopics fall afoul of Aristotle's wisdom about aesthetic distance. He

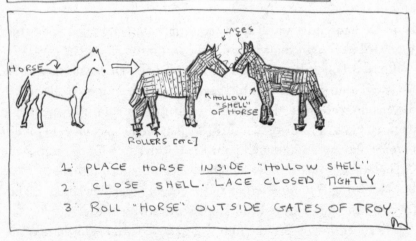

FROM THE TROJAN HORSE COMPETITION —
AN EARLY SUBMISSION.

HORSE

LACES

HOLLOW "SHELL" OF HORSE

ROLLERS [etc]

1: PLACE HORSE INSIDE "HOLLOW SHELL"
2: CLOSE SHELL. LACE CLOSED TIGHTLY.
3: ROLL "HORSE" OUTSIDE GATES OF TROY.

warned against taking the audience out of their role of guests and recasting them as judges.

If one knew the actual work of Frances Farmer, one could only say, of *any* impersonation: a) Yes, that's just like her; or b) No, that's not a bit like her.

Each takes the audience out of the moment.

You might object, what if one did *not* know the real Frances? In that case, why in the world make a film about her? If the film were a good drama it would succeed absent the announced impersonation; if not, the character's name would make no difference.

Do see the true Frances Farmer (*Son of Fury*, *South of Pago Pago*, *Come and Get It*). She was an impossibly lovely, brilliant actress, her performances so true and *odd* that one blinks at the first moment, thinking, What, then, is *this* . . . ?; and then one can't get enough of her. You think afterward, Oh, *I* see. *That* was acting.

In this Miss Farmer was the equal of the greatest of the great, the biggest star on Broadway in 1923 and then in the movies, Jeanne Eagels.

Eagels went from the stage to the silents, and then to sound, making only *The Letter* and *Jealousy*.

*The Letter*, remade with Bette Davis in the Eagels role, is a lesson in the difference between talent and genius. Jeanne died young, of drugs and alcohol, and Frances of cancer, after a life of alcoholism and depression. May they rest in peace.


We in Show Business are like our Brothers, the Criminals, and theirs, the Politicians. Discarded or aged-out, we can never go straight. Their racket, like ours, is their life; supplying excitement, comradeship, and the possibility of gain, glory, and fame. For us in Show Biz these were always just one lucky break away.

The rooms at Versailles were tiny, unventilated, filthy, and dark, but the Nobility considered any other habitation exile.

\* \* \*

See: the self-proclaimed Socially Conscious. Translation, "arrogant"; for all people are conscious of their society. The phrase capitalized means ". . . to the exclusion of acknowledging the possibility of any alternative positions."

The Socially Conscious, I say, want to use films to "do good." But the lesson of the dramatist is that *no* one acts from the desire to do wrong. Each person thinks his acts good. The addict cycles between withdrawal, remorse, resolution, and reversion. Each step, in its time, is understood by him as the ultimate good. The wife-killer himself is, during the act, more assured of its rectitude than he is of any other thing in his life.*

Those of us capable of assessing our actions truthfully must conclude, from time to time, that we were wrong. In the healthy person this leads to remorse, shame, regret, and perhaps then to resolution.

Watching the good comedy or drama, we are very much ahead of the misguided protagonist. We can appreciate his fall, as he is other than we; our appreciation is heightened by the simultaneous knowledge that we are the same.

Melodrama is the useful (and pleasing) removal of that second perception.

Here we know that the Villain is *not* an aspect of the Hero (OURSELVES) but a complete other. We knew him of old by his Black Mustache, or his Black Hat; and today by his white skin. Or he may be fantasized as a Supervillain or monster, his signs of evilness many wings, or arms, or the blue-screen display of his Awesome Power to produce discomfort.

The historic "You must pay the rent," "I *can't* pay the rent," "Well, then I shall tie you to the railroad track" becomes, in today's

---

* My favorite New York story. Nineteen eighty-five, two sculptors, Carl Andre and his wife, Ana Mendieta, quarreled. The neighbors heard the screaming. They lived on the thirty-fourth floor, and she took the quick way down to the ground level. He called 911 and said, "We had a quarrel about the fact that I was more exposed to the public than she was and she went to the bedroom and I went after her, and she went out of the window." Genius.

ANNALS OF EXECUTIVE THOUGHT: THE SEQUEL

shake-and-bake tentpole, "Or I shall destroy the world, with my secret Power of _____."

Who are these, our own Village Idiots, the suits of Hollywood, insisting on the audience's need for animated renditions of Norse Sagas?* Their films are made for the Youth, and the Youth love fantasies of power. I myself was fair addicted to comic books.

The Execs of today are yes-persons at one with the voters who ban schoolyard dodgeball as too violent. At the awards, Hollywood cries out against Violence, otherwise making its living by its depiction.

To add to the enormity, the guns in films are wrong. One cannot

---

* If you put cilantro on it, Californians will eat cat shit.

silence a revolver; a revolver *has* no safety. A Colt .45 or a semi-automatic must be cocked in order to shoot *or* threaten. *And.* No one in film *ever* recorks the bottle after pouring a drink. What drinker (actor or character) would do that? And yet we do not object.

No character in a film getting shaved by a barber ever finished the shave. He was always called away in its midst, wiping his half-shorn face of the lather.

And my bête noire: no film Judge, gaveling the room to order, and threatening in its absence to Clear the Court, has ever cleared the court. I'd watch a film of *only* the Judge Clearing the Court.

The male characters in classic films are always guzzling milk. They order milk in bars, to show they are good. I just don't like it. Too much pointless milk.

# CURIOUS SURVIVALS

Telegraphists developed great skill in transmission of Morse code, but when voice transmission superseded Morse their skill was useless. Of use to them, in the transition period, however, was their proximity to the new technology.

The telegraphist's skill was manipulation and interpretation of one simple key—in effect, an on-off switch; but Radio and Voice required understanding and skill in electronics.

Telegraphist lore survived in operator lingo, 23 = I have to go, enshrined as 23 skidoo, of the twenties, meaning get lost. Eighty-six = no further, in bar lingo, no more drinks; SOS, the universal signal for "I require help," this last the final echo of the telegraphists.

Why this and not that?

The whole damn thing is a mystery and, like them all, gets lost in a future that, in addition to being ignorant of the facts, couldn't care less—right around the bend, the demise not only of knowledge of the telegraphists but of the awareness of their lore in hobbyist anthropologists who cherish it as arcana.

This, as I understand it, is Time.

Cockney rhyming slang was an in-group lingo. It differs from pig latin in that it was a language rather than a code. PL is a simple transition, rhyming slang was all invention, its neologisms adopted for their poetic or humorous worth.

Trouble and strife for *wife*; bottle and glass for *arse*; God forbids, *kids*, *godfors*—what a treat, rhymes found for words and then mutilated.

I mention *twist*. Abe Reles (1906–1941), a noted gangster, was known as Kid Twist because of his fondness for the ladies. *Twist* was a contemporary term for a girl. It's now held to be derogatory, perhaps because of Reles's hobby, but it was only rhyming slang: twist and twirl = girl.

A student of language (myself) might note the opprobrium attached to Twist as somehow *directly* insulting, assuming that the word has some connotation unfriendly to the female disposition or anatomy (how?); thus are we suckered past understanding into prejudice. This is, of course, inevitable, as who has the time to dissect all human behavior and speech searching for final clarity? Q. Who knows what evil lurks in the hearts of men? A. The Shadow Knows. MWAAAhahahahah! In this he is preeminent, if not, in fact, alone.

Of rude speech: I made my early reputation and living by my use of the vernacular. But my internal Nice Jewish Boy is still affronted by "this sucks" and "your night in the barrel," two phrases in genteel and universal use connoting fellatio.

Baseball's next-up batter is described as *on deck*, and that following him as *in the hole*; hole is, of course, *hold*; the phrases are clearly nautical.

The square shades, used in controlling light onstage were known, for their opacity, as Blacks; they are now called *solids*, and "White" has become an epithet.

Mrs. (missus), was originally an honorific applied to a woman irrespective of her marital status; it is an abbreviation for Mistress. It was later taken up as a designation of honor for a married woman. Gloria Steinem insisted that there should be a marriage-neutral term for women, and we now have Ms., with Mrs. seen by the Left as an insult.

Gender-specific designations are the "fightin' words" of today's corporate coteries. The fraidy-cats of Film notable among them. Best Boy (the second position in the electrical department) was a position and term worthy of respect, applied even when women began filling that position, and accepted, by them, as an in-group irony. Today the job is known as Head Gaffer.*

But D-girl, a development person, seems to be used for job holders of any sex whatever. And my beloved friend Meg is a teamster, and I refer to her as "My Teamstress." She, like most teamsters I know, has a sense of humor.

Here's a game we played on the set of *Phil Spector* (2013). The challenged were required to reply to any statement in Teamster. This speech was limited to the job's three responses: Whoa, Hey, and Alright.

Q. You go out last night?
A. *Whoa* . . .
Q. What do you think of Borges?
A. . . . *hey* . . .
Q. Your mother's a whore.
A. Alright.

Lordy, we had fun on *Phil Spector*. It was the summer of Anthony Weiner. The *Post* and the *Daily News* competed, day by day, with headlines sufficient to save All Journalism from disgrace. "Weiner Still Standing Up," "Weiner Sticks It Out," "Give Weiner a Hand," etcetera. He, it will be remembered, was a Congressman or something, disgraced for the online self-pornography issued under his nom de guerre, Carlos Danger.

In New York, we had an ongoing hurricane, and an earthquake sufficient to clear the set as we scurried for cover. Bette Midler was injured and had to leave the show, and Helen Mirren gave up her vacation in Spain to fly in on two days' notice and replace her. Al Pacino played Phil, and Helen his defense counsel, modeled on Linda

---

* Enlisted Air Force personnel of both sexes are referred to as Airmen, a tradition with no ill effects.

Kenney Baden; her on-screen partner was played by Jeffrey Tambor, the funniest man who ever lived.

He delivered one of my lines, disparaging some idea, with an accompanying motion. I said "cut," and Helen asked him, "What does that gesture represent?" "Helen," he said, "that's masturbating." "No, Jeffrey," she said, "*this* is masturbating," and made an entirely different gesture. *

We know that should the tail become smarter than the dog it will wag its host. The phenomenon is obvious not only to victims but to sentient observers of bureaucracy.

Teddy Roosevelt instituted the Civil Service in 1883, to cure the ills of the spoils system. One hundred and change years on, the Civil Service unions possess the clout to strong-arm the government.

Like any prosperous bureaucracy, a Nation or a Rich Man's Estate, bureaucrats in Movies will appoint subordinates. In the atmosphere of plenty, and without supervision, these will engage in graft, empire building, and chicane. They're free to do so, as they have little else to occupy their time. Those above them are not only busy with their *own* schemes but happy to display attendants, whose number indicates the boss's power.

Early movies indubitably required scripts. These had to be purchased and churned out, as the audience was waiting. That a script might have "worth" was, of course, important, but its worth consisted, back then, solely in its immediate accessibility to a waiting cameraman.

---

* My daughter Clara, age sixteen, was a production assistant (dogsbody) on the set. She was out all night holding down the perimeter, running for coffee, and generally living the old Cowboy Adage: if you join the Cattle Drive, sleep in the winter. When we wrapped, she'd been promoted to Head Transport PA. It was time for her return to high school, but she said she couldn't abandon the crew during wrapping out. A triumph of Film Culture. She came back to L.A., dropped out of high school, and did two years of acting as the "human child" on the ABC sitcom *The Neighbors*. She then wrote, directed, and starred in a film that went to Tribeca; this, today's Jewish improvement on "My son, the Doctor."

Later, Golden Age studios staffed rooms full of writers, some of whose work was Not Needed on Voyage. Prolonged prosperity suggested more layers of waste (and thus of the display of prestige).

Producers of every sub-description (Co-, Executive, Supervising, Co-Executive, and so on) emerged to oversee (that is, batten on) the Development Process. As no film ever emerged from the Development Process, it held great possibility for display of waste.

Actual films could only employ a limited (if large) number of drones, but a process that made nothing could direct any number to pursue that goal.

The Development Process created the "girlfriend-as-executive." This is not to disparage women, either as employees or drones, nor to dispute their right to either position. But I will comment on the Job Description. "D-girl," a term currently in use. (D standing for Development.)

Why the "girl"? As the job evolved from the old studio heads' weekend habit of handing the scripts (which they never read) to their young friends. In effect: "Here, feel important, I'm going to take a nap." (I wrote a play about it, *Speed-the-Plow*.)

The D-girls make a living ensuring that no scripts that pass their desks get made. If their operations were limited to endorsing filmable scripts, they'd be out of a job. (Only two hundred to three hundred films a year are actually made in Hollywood. They are greenlit based upon the marketability of cast, director, and franchise. *None* of them is made because some underling endorsed a script.)

Well, all that lives must breathe (Lord Byron), and an organization is an organism and not a machine. Its life strives to continue and grow; and both growth *and* decay will attract parasites.

These, the development folks, Diversity Capos, and so on, are subsumed within the host organism; but there is another class, offering not support but proximity—in effect, like sex therapists following the camp followers who are trailing the caravan.

These offer classes in scriptwriting, auditioning, voice, résumé writing, and so on. As if the Persian caravans, unable to accommodate more hetairas and eunuchs, offered "Eunuch Workshops" to the folks who couldn't make the trip.

How does one Break into the Movies?

Ted Morgan in *On Becoming American* observed that Americans speak of "getting a break,"* but that the concept is foreign to Europeans, who assume that success might only come through application and persistence.

How might one persist in a hopeless task without losing hope? By ensuring that the task is endless—that, in our case, a screenplay could be infinitely perfectible, kept in "development" till the cows come home, with regular meetings with the assigned executive, and repeated returns to the computer with yet another load of notions. Or perhaps an aspirant has not yet gotten to a D-girl but is making the rounds, offering his script to anyone self-proclaimed as a producer. These attempts will come to nothing but eventual disenchantment on the part of the self-proclaimed, as the original script, given his notes, becomes less and less distinguishable from mud.

Should this producer decamp, the aspiring writer will seek out another before whom to throw his wares, and this fellow will begin with a whole other parade of notes. By this time the writer has, himself, sickened of the project, but how to disengage? He cannot, for then he must recognize he has failed. So his "work on the script" may go on for years. See Mark Twain's *The Gilded Age*, where an aspirant trying to build a dam or something, spends a lifetime in Washington, always just one lunch away from success.

*       *       *

---

* "Now and then a 'lucky strike' or an 'excellent prospect' gladdened the miners' hearts, but most of the time they felt sorry for themselves." On the California gold rush, from *A Shovel of Stars*, by Ted Morgan.

Hollywood is where Nope Springs Eternal, and yet they come, my like, inseparable from the addiction as the stuck 'n' steaming gambler who points to his few remaining chips and says, to his pleading spouse, "Just wait till I lose *this*."

Everyone wants to get into the act. And always did. Film Schools, actually unrelated to the moviemaking process, may trace their descent from fan clubs; and this book, actually, is a descendant of the Movie Mag.

AWARDS SCREENERS:
THE BIZ GOES GREEN

FOR YOUR CONSIDERATION

Bloffordt
...a Victorian Romance...

BOTH THE PACKAGING AND THE ARTISTIC CONTENT OF THIS FILM HAVE BEEN RECYCLED

FLUGBUMP MULTIMEDIA

# THE FRANK SINATRA STORY

I met Tina Sinatra at a Sue Mengers soiree. She paid me the great compliment of saying I reminded her of her father. I asked Sue later if this was just pleasantry on Tina's part, and Sue said, "No, she meant it."

I always adored Frank's acting. He never made *anything* up. See him as the Parish Priest in *The Miracle of the Bells* and then as the Major in *The Manchurian Candidate*.

If that were not enough, he, as the Chairman of the Board, that is, the Motengator, is the point of the Don Rickles story.

Don rose to fame through Insult Comedy. He got his break as a lounge comic in Vegas.

He saw Frank entering the joint and approached him humbly. "Mr. Sinatra," he said, "I'm no one, but could I ask a favor. I'm playing here, and my wife is with me. It's her birthday. If, on your way out, you could stop at our table and simply say, 'Hi there, Don.' It would make her day." Sinatra said nothing and walked on.

When he left the casino, he stopped by Don's table.

"Hi, Don," he said.

"Fuck you, Frank," Rickles said.

Frank dissolved, screaming with laughter, and Don was made.

I worked with Don on *The Unit* (Season 2, Episode 13); and I asked him, "*Tateleh*: the Frank Sinatra story . . . ?" "My hand to God," he said.

Don's gag had a precedent in the ancient tradition of the Court Jester. While the Monarch received adulation, his Jester sat behind him, whispering.

It is recorded that he whispered, "Remember, you are just a man," but I suspect his riff was closer to the bone. Why? As anyone could whisper the one phrase—or its like—how would one choose a Jester, which, we must assume, was a coveted job, in any case better than currying sheep or whatever the proles did.

The Jester must have been chosen for his ability to *drive home* the healthy lesson in acceptable form, which is to say through comedy. Its simple repetition quickly would have become wallpaper. No, the Jester must have been a comic, getting his job *exactly* as Don Rickles did.

The Great, when told "Remember you are just a man," *congratulate* themselves on their preternatural ability to accept criticism; but a jester who could *stick* it to them, who actually brought them up short, and made 'em like it, was worth something. E.g.:

"Five of your concubines say you're a rotten lay."

"If you fuck up this Triumphant Parade like you fucked up Sicily, I'm looking for another job."

"Wave, dickhead, that's what you're paid for."

Now, some of the Caesars may understandably have resented the actual reminders as impertinence, and then had their jesters killed. (See what Ed Sullivan did to Jackie Mason.)* And the jesters, on the line, were betting the ranch on their ability to know the Room. Thus the birth of stand-up comedy.

I wrote a one-act play, some time back, *Keep Your Pantheon*, about a troupe of the worst actors in ancient Rome. Ed O'Neill played its star, Strabo. An example:

"Hello to the Tenth African Legion, they're the boys, their spears come in three sizes, small, medium, and 'Thank you for a lovely evening.' And Hello to Marcus Quintus, who, you know, has just made the switch from Boys to Women . . . The fellow who used to think the clitoris was a building in Greece. We heard, on his wedding night, he said, 'I know it's around here *somewhere* . . .'"

---

* Sullivan destroyed his career by insisting Jackie made an obscene gesture on Ed's TV show.

We may recognize something as amusing, which bears the same relationship to comedy that Twinkies bear to food. But a laugh, like a lascivious glance, cannot be recalled. If the Monarch laughed, the Jester had not only saved his life but earned his keep. If the Monarch turned red, it may have been "*sauve qui peut.*"

Today, who are the souls who, when they go out, are like Don Rickles, playing each time for all the marbles? There seem to be a few; and you, like me, will have your favorites. But the climate, and the curse, of the times is sententiousness, our culture now screaming "unclean" at anything that might, in some notional person's estimation, hurt some other person's feelings. The Jester, behind the King, is now constantly aware that One Wrong Word will mean the end of his career.

After some brief thought, I've decided to include some actually provocative words and pictures in this book. It's a bit like extensive dentistry—at my age, it's ridiculous to have long-term preventative work done. I have no idea what a "legacy" is, but I do know that its pursuit can lead to no work worthy of even momentary notice.

Jerry Lewis and Red Skelton both performed disability as comedy—Jerry miming Muscular Dystrophy, and Red, some sort of Moronism. They were hugely successful, but are unwatchable today.

Lenny Bruce brought the whole thing up short and called the Government down on him, for saying the unsayable.

In my home, Chicago, he got tossed out of town for saying, of the slain and dismembered victim of our Leopold and Loeb, "Bobby Franks was a snotty kid." The cops were called to his show and testified that, additionally, he used the epithet "mother" as "half-a-word."

And the great Sarah Silverman got tossed out of Canada for saying at the Montreal Comedy Festival: "I am now going to recite in one-half minute a list of the Vice Presidents of the United States. Backward. But I need two things: I need absolute silence, and I need to stick my thumb in my vagina."

Latterly, John Oliver said of the late Queen: "We have to start with the UK, which is clearly still reeling from the shocking death of a ninety-six-year-old woman by natural causes . . ."

This is the opposite of hordes stacking teddy bears outside of Buckingham Palace, the bear somehow commemorating the late Princess Diana.

An allied joke, and I would most happily credit the author, if I knew his identity.*

Grace Kelly, our beloved Queen of the Shiksas, married Prince Rainier of Monaco.

Years later she died in a car crash. An equerry was assigned to break the news. "Your Highness, I have good news and bad news. The bad news is that your wife is dead. The good news is that the Mercedes will be fixed by Thursday."

The Jester's *job* was to offend. Like Don, Sarah Silverman, and Lenny.

The purpose of comedy is to expose our folly.

Television's Situation Comedies of yore have become the sole comedies of today.

Why are they not amusing? Because a joke must be about disorder, and a situation comedy is about a *situation*, which is to say continuation; the mixture as before; "everything is fine, *however, uh*, oh . . . the painters put the wallpaper on upside down, and the trees have their roots at the top, and your boss is coming for dinner." So what?

Frank Sinatra had all the money, fame, and companionship anyone could desire. What could one give him that *he* would value? A laugh. And, better, a laugh about himself.

---

* My friend Jonathan Katz created the Freudian Slip joke: "This morning at breakfast with my father I meant to say, 'Pass the toast,' and it came out, 'Yousonofabitch, you ruined my childhood.'" I, and you, have heard the joke in many forms, it's his joke, but how would one know who *didn't* know—his reward being its inclusion in our Culture. I wrote the polar bear joke for him.

Young polar bear comes home from school, he says, "Mom, am I actually a polar bear?" "Yes." "I mean, are you and Dad polar bears?" "Yes." "Then, I'm a full polar bear?" "Yes, why do you ask?" "Because I'm fucking freezing."

New-speak slogans suggesting we "embrace our humanity" are inducements to self-congratulation. But we scream with laughter at the recognition that our beloved "humanity" is a joke. Our laugh is the recognition that no one is here but us chickens.

A favorite Barbara story:

After a day of shooting we went to the sound mix.

The studio door was opened by an ancient guard. He walked us down the hall past large framed photos of silent film stars. We passed Lillian Gish, Douglas Fairbanks, Mary Pickford, and he pointed to the image of a very handsome man dressed as a gaucho.

"You know who that is?" he said.

"Ramon Novarro," I said.

"You know how he died?"

"Yes," I said, "his boyfriend beat him to death with a dildo."

He nodded. "His boyfriend beat him to death with a dildo," he said. He looked around, beckoned me closer and leaned in. "He had a boyfriend," he whispered. "Because he was a homo."

# HIGH & LOW

I was hired to rewrite a rather bad film, *We're No Angels* (1989). The original (1955) starred Bogey and was directed by Michael Curtiz (*Casablanca*). It was mawkish, but presold as A Christmas Film.

In my version, Bob De Niro and Sean Penn are to star as two escaped convicts. So far, so good. And the Irishman Neil Jordan is to direct. He later rose to prominence with *The Crying Game*, a film that the audience left, satisfied, as it revealed that the Lead Girl had a penis.

I wrote a smashing script. The Producer, someone or other, flew to Cambridge for a meeting between me and Neil Jordan, who flew from Ireland.

We were introduced, "Hi, hi," and Neil said, "I have some questions about your script." I riposted, "Then why don't you go fuck yourself." And got up and left.

The revenge, if not his, then of the gods, was that the film (in contradistinction to the script) Just Wasn't Funny. And there I was, paid in full.

Oh Lord, the films I've been fired from.

Martin Scorsese, who I'd turned down for *Raging Bull*, asked me to rewrite Kurosawa's *High and Low* (1963).

This is a pretty swell kidnap story. The rich guy, our hero, is Toshiro Mifune. His son was at summer camp with the chauffeur's kid. Mifune's son gets kidnapped, and the kidnapper says, "Five million bucks, or I kill the kid."

This taps out Mifune, but he of course says he'll pay. The chauffeur offers to contribute his *own* life savings. Then Mifune's son walks in, and we find it was the chauffeur's kid they snatched. All rejoice, as all has ended well. Then the kidnapper calls to say the deal still stands, five mil for the *chauffeur's* kid.

"Well," Toshiro's wife says, "of course, you don't have to pay." But he says, "The chauffeur was going to give me his life savings for *my* kid . . ." Drama ensues, and then falls apart in Kurosawa's last act.

In the last act, the drama turns into a procedural, playing past the essential question.

The film was based on one of Ed McBain's 87th Precinct novels. Ed couldn't figure the end out either. I figured it out.

In my third act, the Hero's threatened by his wife, by the board of the company he runs, and by everybody and their aunt—"stand down, let the cops try to find the kid, walk away from it, you do not have to pay for another man's kid"—and here is my contribution: his kid then says the same thing. He tells his father that it is not his responsibility to ransom the other kid, his best friend, a boy he himself has betrayed, by leaving him to the kidnappers.

Our hero escapes from his home, where his wife is trying to restrain him from paying the ransom. He takes his son *with* him and directs the *boy* to pay the ransom to the kidnappers, expunging his guilt by an act of courage.

Our hero and his son then return to the house. The son goes to his mother and Mifune sequesters himself with the cops. Later, he asks the maid for his son.

"He's gone," she says. "Your wife took him." Our guy says, "He'll come back."

How did I figure it out?

In the denouement, Kurosawa inserts a Technicolor sequence in the black-and-white film. The kidnapper is supposed to make smoke from a chimney, to reveal his location. The film goes to color. Oooh and ahh, certainly, but what does it indicate, save that Akira knew (if only subconsciously) that something was lacking and he'd better take up the slack?

Well, something *was* lacking; a correct denouement.

Of what? Well, it would have to be of a problem or objective.

What was the Hero's objective?

He came up from the Assembly Line, he became Head of the Company, he's about to take the company Public and become very rich, then his kid gets kidnapped.

The third act and the punch line *must* be an elaboration of the central issue, ending in its resolution through a new understanding of the problem. The new understanding can only come about through the missteps (Acts One and Two) of the Hero. What is at issue? Our most prominent hint is the kidnapping of his son.

In the third act, then, he *must* be striving to do something for his son. But. His son is already home.

What is the solution—it baffled Ed McBain and Kurosawa. No shame in that, I've been stymied myself. But I was being paid to figure it out and so, I, like the Hero (now my doppelgänger), had to find the solution.

Act One. He rises from the Assembly Line. How in the world would that have to do with his son?

Ah. He marries poor and WANTS TO GIVE HIS SON A BET-TER LIFE.

How did I come to this conclusion?

I began with the assumption that, as the signal event is the kid's kidnapping, the story *must* be about the Hero and his kid.

Act Two, then, he is about to Go Public, and become vastly wealthy, thus *fulfilling* his responsibilities to his family, now almost on Easy Street. His kid gets kidnapped, returns, and all the household counsels the Hero that he need not ransom the other kid. He is unsure, and considers their arguments, UNTIL HIS OWN KID PUTS THEM FORTH. ("Dad, you aren't under an obligation to the chauffeur's kid.")

With this moment, the film's throughline reveals itself. In his struggle to provide, first, sustenance and, then, luxury for his son, he has *ruined* him, to the point where the son now prefers money to the life of his best friend. Our hero, thus, goes to ransom the other kid, *primarily* to save his own son. How? He takes his son to the kidnappers and sends *him* in to ransom the other kid. And so the story is solved.

As you can see, I was pleased with this solution. This, as always with a correct solution, leads one to observe, "It was there *all along*."* (This is actually the definition of a correct solution.)

Great script. Scott Rudin was producing, and Mike Nichols was going to direct. I was called to the (inevitable) conference about, as usual, the "piece of shit" I'd written. We conferred at Mike's Fifth Avenue penthouse.

Out on the terrace, across from the Metropolitan Museum, we were served a superb lunch by a perfect, uniformed staff. Mike and Scott hated my script.

Me: "Why?"

They: "It has to be about *greed*. He needs to be punished because of his greed."

There we are, surrounded by Picassos, two *ungeschtupped* (very wealthy) showfolk—Jews, like me, risen from The Gutter to perfectly deserved comfort and acclaim.

"Fellas," I said, "it has nothing to *do* with greed."

"No, no," they said, slurping their blinis with caviar (I swear), "he has to be punished for his greed."

I finished my white wine and left. I regret that I did *not* say: "Are you two kikes out of your fucking minds . . ." as the introduction to a brilliant speech. You, reader, may imagine it, and I assure you the actual diatribe would have been *even better*.

But I knew that such a speech would have availed me little save my own self-amusement. Why? Scott is, and Mike was, very far from stupid. Both loved the movies and knew them from Méliès to the

---

* Zanuck and Brown fired me off of *The Verdict* and hired Jay Allen to write a new script. Sidney Lumet read both and told them he was doing mine. We all were nominated and went to the Oscars, and Dick Zanuck threw his arm around me and said, "We had it *all along* . . ." This is the same Dick Zanuck who later fired me off *Lolita*, saying of my script, "You made him seem like a pedophile."

present day. But, *but*, both were of Old Hollywood, and nobody in Hollywood ever changed his mind.*

Why not?

Because they don't know why it works. (It being the script.)†

There is, certainly, a magic about performances. Some actors illumine the screen, and one will watch them forever, doing *whatever* they're doing. Some (actually) seem to have no life behind the eyes. We can't say why. But a script *can be analyzed*. The question is not "Why doesn't the *movie* work?" but "Why doesn't the script?" If it does *not* work, it can, and must, be fixed. Most script doctoring is addressed piecemeal, that is, a car chase, a snappy line, a love scene *here* might recapture the audience's attention.

This is the understanding of an amateur. The Professional (myself) addresses the script as a problem in construction—just as the magician plots an effect. Everything leading to the effect must be

---

* In Ted Morgan's *Maugham*, he tells the story of the casting of *The Razor's Edge*. This, you may remember, was Maugham's grand novel about a young WWI flyer who cannot return to his prewar life but goes off to discover himself. The film starred Tyrone Power as the flyer, Gene Tierney as the Rich Girl who abandons him when he won't return to society, and Anne Baxter as the Nice Girl. She marries a rich fella who loses all in the crash; and she turns to drink and becomes a whore.

Darryl Zanuck was producing. Anne Baxter was put up for the film, but, according to Maugham's story, Zanuck didn't find her sexy. He was at his pool one afternoon with Gregory Ratoff, who said she was a great lay, and Zanuck changed his mind.

In any case, that's the story. She's great in the film. Anne Baxter was Frank Lloyd Wright's granddaughter. They were taken on a tour of Disney in the '30s. Walt walked them through the labs and showed them the early "storyboard," stick figure animation of the whale scene from *Pinocchio*. Then they watched the finished product, and Frank said, show the *other* one.

† Hollywood is hierarchical and savage. Those dealing with their inferiors may express an opinion, and the opinion may be disputed. But they are simultaneously proclaiming a *position*, criticism of which by an inferior is cause for dismissal.

clear to the audience—so that they will lead *themselves* to that place where they can be delighted or awed by the disruption of their mental processes, the Revelation, "It was there all the time."

The failed magician may say, "Yes, *but*, I worked *so* hard on it" all day long, but the audience will be the judge of that, and if he wants to advance from Birthday Parties he will study to put himself in their place.

Mike and Scott, delightful companions, enjoyed their adventure in screenwriting; the film never got made, but they congratulated themselves on their superiority to greed. "Lads," I thought, "you worked for it, you deserve it, you have nothing to be ashamed of, and should enjoy yourselves and be proud." But apparently *they* didn't think so. Or, at least, had some ambivalence. I miss Mike. Everyone does. And I always enjoy being with Scott, who loves movies. But when the big winner knows it's too early to leave the table with his winnings and decides to hoard them till he can, reasonably, go home, he *will* start losing, as he's no longer playing poker.

ANNALS OF EXECUTIVE THOUGHT #2

**MEMO**

okay. we get the same
team that did "The
Crying Game" — they
remake "Black Beauty".
Half way through the
film they take off
his saddle, and
discover HE'S
A COW !!!
　　　　　H.

**MIRAMAX**

# VILLAINS AND SEXUAL ABUSE
# AT THE GOLDEN GLOBES

As a cute young thing, I danced in the Maurice Chevalier show *Toutes Voiles Dehors*, at Expo '67. I am the last person alive to have been onstage with Maurice Chevalier, whom many in postwar France considered a villain. He was indicted as a collaborator, and a bunch of folks wanted to hang him.*

The only other villains with whom I was associated in Show Business were, of course, the producers and Studio Folk. I worked, however, with some grand on-screen villains. Notably, two great comics.

Steve Martin played the villain in my film *The Spanish Prisoner*; Tim Allen played the villain in *Redbelt*. I always loved comics playing straight. There is no better performance than Jackie Gleason's in *The Hustler*, and Jerry Lewis redeemed a career as a buffoon in Scorsese's *The King of Comedy*.

The grandest villain of all, a testament to genius, was the light bulb, HAL, in *2001: A Space Odyssey*.

For two afternoons, Kubrick was my phone pal. I'd written *On Directing Film* and sent it to him, ostensibly a gesture of respect but actually a begging letter, looking for a quote. He called me from his home in England. We spoke for two afternoons, mostly about guns. He was a competitive pistol shot; I was too. I of course wanted to steer the conversation to film gossip, but firearms, like aviation and

---

* Cf. the great Arletty, whose boyfriend was head of the Paris Gestapo. Arraigned for treason after the war, she testified, "My heart is French, my pussy is International." They let her off. *This* is why I love the French.

sexual dish among their aficionados, trump all. He did tell me that Kirk Douglas was a pain in the ass on *Spartacus*, and that, on his first meeting re: *Dr. Strangelove*, Peter Sellers came to the door dressed as Hitler, and kept it up, accent and all, through a long London brunch.

I asked Kubrick about Sue Lyon's introductory shot in *Lolita*. I said it was swell that he'd blown the background out, that is, overlit the shot, so she appears in a haze of light. He said I'd just seen a bad print.

His *The Killing* was my inspiration for the first film I wrote and directed, *House of Games*. There I was, in Santa Barbara, on location while Bob Rafelson shot *Postman*. I'd bought a 1969 Karmann Ghia off the street in L.A. and commuted in it, weekends, down the coast, listening to the radio.

And there was Glenn Gould playing Bach, the C-minor Toccata. It is the ultimate elaboration of a simple triad—that is, of three notes. Jerry Kern did something similar in "Ol' Man River." I pulled over to the side of Highway 1 to listen to the exquisite intricacies extracted from a simple theme, and one thing led to another, and I wrote a movie.

Beginning with a noir gave me a taste for the thing, which played into a strength: the ability to craft a plot. This was not a natural skill (like writing dialogue, a gift, for which I will take all the undeserved credit on offer) but rather laudable as a test of determination. As Trollope wrote, "It's dogged as does it." In a noir one *must* stay ahead of the audience, the inclusion of the obligatory scene stops it dead, and the audience goes to the concession stand.

The comics inspire, as The Joke is the perfect paradigm for a dramatic plot, which is, formally, just a joke extended. The solution to each must surprise and delight *as* it is revealed as inevitable.

Steve and Tim, obvious good guys, turn out, in my films, to be baddies, and we may be surprised. If they were obvious malefactors, waxed mustache or its emotional equivalent, there would be no punch line.

We might say that Kubrick's aperçu was an anticipation of the computer-as-villain; but his filmic villain was NOT EVEN a computer, it was a light bulb which we were *informed* was a computer. And that is genius.

We all know that our truest opponents are the swine who take advantage of our good nature slash stupidity. We defend ourselves against obvious threats, but aggressors study to attack us through the undefended points. That's logic.

The Germans came through Belgium in World War I and almost took Paris. The French built the impregnable Maginot Line, extending right up to and just short of the Belgian defenses. The Germans struck again, in 1940, in Belgium, and this time took Paris, full stop.

The baddies in Hollywood, on first meeting, smile—why not?, it costs them nothing and plays to our vanity and greed. Who is immune? (Gandhi himself had thirty-one different loincloths, one for each day of the month.) Sexual titillation, like most passions, is fungible: this can be mistaken or traded for that (see sadomasochism).

The ambitious come to Hollywood, excited by the promise of reward, and, heck, since they're there *anyway*, may trade sex for the promise. As with the disappointed flea market vendor at the close of the day, it makes little sense to cart it home.

The old tale has the young thing, fresh from Kansas, invited to a meeting at a producer's apartment. She arrives at ten a.m., he greets her, clad only in a bathrobe, and the bed unmade. She writes in shock to her mom back home. "Imagine," she writes, "ten o'clock and the *bed unmade*."

I'd have thought the young things criminally doltish (old joke: Ann-Margret is the only girl in Hollywood who still has her hyphen), until came the dawn. There I was, at my biannual visit to the Golden Globes. The gag was that one showed up, sat at various tables full of stringers (reporters paid only on acceptance of submissions) from newspapers with unfamiliar names situated in countries of which no one had heard, and mimed personability.

One of the Head Dogs of the outfit greeted me as an old friend, did we not meet once every two years, when I'd appear and get my picture took and flog another magnificent film which his peripatetic coterie would fail to endorse? This Head Dog was effusive in his thanks for my appearance and became overly so. For as we spoke he, perhaps absent-mindedly, stuck his hand down my pants.

The conversation continued for a beat or two, as I realized, ". . . *hold* on, here . . ." and put some daylight between us.

What had I done to "lead him on"? Was I "inviting"? No. Was I that cute? No. What had he found attractive? Ah, I reflected that night, he *must* have been turned on by the excellence of my film!

In which I was close-to-at-one with generations of the (self-) seduced-and-abandoned dead blondes, rough trade, and regular old aspirants.

Sadie and Abie have been married fifty-five years. She's dying in the hospital, he goes to visit, she asks him to "throw a little schtup into her," he does so. The next day, she rises from her deathbed, cured. He begins to weep. "I could have saved Eleanor Roosevelt."

I love Eleanor Roosevelt.

LOST IMAGES OF AMERICAN MUSIC. FROM HER "GARAGE BAND" PERIOD.

ELEANOR ROOSEVELT AND THE CROTON-ON-HUDSON SEX KITTENS (1904)

I wrote a smashing police script (fired from), in which an old cop tells a rookie, "You may be broke and tired and wet, but you're going to get more pussy than Eleanor Roosevelt."

Speaking of which, I wrote a television pilot about two con men flogging a counterfeit letter proving beyond a doubt that Abraham Lincoln was gay.

Yes, the business changed (died), and as I aged out of it *and* got sidelined because of my politics (respect for the Constitution, etc.), my work began to resemble that of the postwar Trobriand Islanders. They'd become fat and sassy during the war, from the air bases built on their islands. Japan surrendered, the Allies and their planes went home, and the islanders constructed large plane-shaped structures out of bamboo, to lure the fellows back.

My equivalent can be seen in the various unproduced works of worth holding my bookends apart.

When I realized that the Globes folk weren't going to give me no stinking statuettes without I forked over *something*, the light bulb went on. I fantasized that, on my next film release, I would go back to their photo-fest and threaten that if they didn't give me a prize I'd have them all deported.

And would they have even responded to my threat? And now that threat exceeds its shelf life, in this day of vanished borders.*

What was I smoking when I wrote *Wag the Dog*?

We know the main gag is the Prez stages a fake war to distract the voters. Even hipper, though, is that the Albanian attack is going to be staged from Canada.

---

* A beloved joke of my youth:
  Q. What do you call a buccaneer?
  A. A high price to pay for corn.
  Inflation has *destroyed* that joke (and yet we speak of "progress" . . . ).

A song from the film:

I guard the Canadian border
I guard the American dream.

Can you imagine my surprise—let alone my lack of delight—on being informed that the Writers Guild had been awarded another author credit for my script?

The phone rang at my place in Vermont, and Jane Rosenthal, *Wag*'s producer (along with Bob De Niro), told me, outraged, that a panel of the Guild had given first-position credit to someone else.

"Huh," I said. "*What* someone else . . . ?"

"It seems," Jane said, "that there'd been a previous script."

Nobody had mentioned it to me, and it would have made no difference to my work if they had, as I wouldn't have read it. I wrote the thing based on Barry Levinson's "The President is caught in a bind, and decides to stage a fake war."

The Guild had awarded first-position credit to a first-submitted script of which I had no knowledge. I called them, proud of my ability to contain my amazement, and explained the situation. Well, they (I can't remember who, in this case, bore that dread title) said, "Why didn't you submit a précis of your position vis-à-vis the other script?"

"I didn't know there *was* another script," I said.

No help for it, I was told, but to appeal to the Review Committee.

The Review Committee, three writers, ruled me the loser.

Then I got a call from one of the three, who said the other two had not even read the scripts but simply looked at the dates of submission.

I didn't rat this person out but did call the Guild, and asked how many times a credit ruling had been overturned on appeal. They told me they were not permitted to give out that information.

Me: "Why not?"

Writers Guild: (Pause.)

Bad *bad* Writers Guild. And yet I'm still paying dues. To an uncaring idiot bureaucracy that is supposed to exist solely to defend my interests. Perhaps you've had a similar experience.

It was, however, as you might imagine, pleasing to have the title embraced as part of our language.

And I received one medal in my life.

The French government named me a Chevalier de l'Ordre des Arts et des Lettres. It comes with a green medal on a green ribbon, and is known as le Pruneau (the prune). Later, their Consul upbraided me for an episode of my TV show *The Unit*. Here, the Foreign Legion conspires to deprive our military guys, The Unit (Dennis Haysbert,

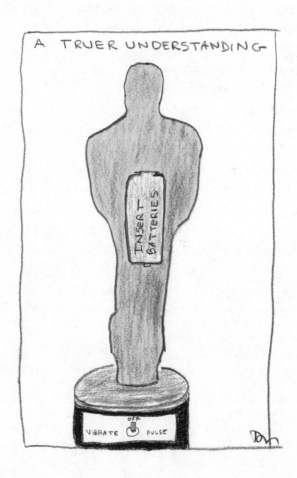

Scott Foley, Max Martini, Demore Barnes, and Michael Irby), of a win. The Guys refer to the Legion lads as Frogs, and Michael Irby announces the appearance of the French to the Team Leader, Dennis, saying, "Hey, Boss: Ribbit."

The Consul wrote I'd impugned the honor of France. Which calls to mind my script *Joan of Bark*. This is a comedy. A young father goes to France to claim some prize or treasure—I believe it is a tapestry of Joan of Arc's dog, Woofy.

Will Ferrell said he'd do it, and it sat around fermenting at Sony for several years. It's still there. I mourn not only the dead script but my unexecuted directorial notions, for the location to which the Hero travels is "downtown Arc," and all the men there wear berets, and the women carry string bags, out of which stick a French Loaf, and are followed by poodles. What a loss.

Old Joke: 1947, upper-class Brit goes to pick up his cleaning and finds the old Jew proprietor weeping.

Brit: What's the matter?

Jew: Ve lost India.

# JOE AND DON

We were shooting *Things Change* on Oak Street Beach in Chicago. This was my mob comedy starring Joe Mantegna and Don Ameche. Don had been the biggest star in Hollywood in '32 and '34 and then, by his admission, was "out of work for two periods of twenty years each."

The second ended when he made *Cocoon* (1985). He'd always played a suave cosmopolitan, his demeanor and accent as universal-unplaceable as Cary Grant's.

Cary grew up, an orphan, in London, and Don was raised by his immigrant father in a bar in Kenosha, Wisconsin. One of his father's friends shot a fellow drinker in the bar. Don's father nodded, took out a stiletto and stabbed his friend in the belly, put the knife in the dead man's hands, and called the cops.

And Joey, of course, came from Cicero.

Joe's Uncle Willie returned a decorated hero of World War II and went to work for various enterprises on the West Side of Chicago. Joe said he'd once landed at O'Hare and gone out to find his Uncle Willie, who'd volunteered to pick him up; and there Willie was, face-down over the hood of his car, handcuffed, and being beaten by the cops. All in good fun, tempers cooled, and Joe asked what happened. Willie explained that the cop had asked him, "Sir, would you please move your car into the designated pickup area?" and he had replied, "Fuck you, you mick cocksucker."*

---

* For years Joe has voiced the character of "Fat Tony" D'Amico on *The Simpsons*, as an homage to his Uncle Willie.

Joe, in addition to being the world's best raconteur, is a story magnet. He reports

Joe and Don got on magnificently; in fact, each was as fine a gentleman as you'd discover on a Hot Summer's Day.

Shel Silverstein and I wrote *Things Change*. We were shooting in Tahoe and Vinny Guastaferro and Joe cooked Italian food, and Don had wines from his L.A. stash flown in for our delight. We were at lunch one day, in pre-production, and a beautiful young woman came up to Joe and explained that she'd always loved his work, and asked what we were doing in Tahoe.

Joe said we were filming and would be there for a month. She said she'd be very pleased to show him around and began to write down her number.

Joe said, "You have an interesting accent. Where are you from?" She said she was from Czechoslovakia.

"Really," Joe said. "My wife's from Czechoslovakia." Pause pause pause. And the young woman went away.

Shel said, "Joe, when that broad says she's from Czechoslovakia, you don't say, 'My wife's from Czechoslovakia.' You *say*, 'I want to knock you down and suck your pussy till you die.'"

Don roared, and I've never heard anyone laugh longer.

I take it back. David Geffen threw a small dinner party for Mike Nichols's seventieth birthday. Eric Idle rose to make a speech. "What could be more enjoyable," he said, "than having your face licked, while ejaculating into the body of a young woman?" The select crowd roared. As we quieted, he began to speak again, and we all thought, No, you can't top it.

However: "I asked my wife, 'Where,' I said, 'where could you find a man equal to Mike in talent, humor, and grace?' 'Hurry up and come,' she said."

Don was eighty during the shoot and spending much of his off-time with one of the crew's young women.

---

he was on the set with a huge star, renowned as a womanizer. They were sitting around, pause, pause, and the star turned to him and said, "If you were a car, what kind of car would you like to fuck?"

And, on the beach, at the last day's shooting, Don became testy, and very testy indeed. It occurred to me that night that of course he was facing the transition, yet again, from deservedly revered film star to Old Man.

Don said, "Joe, you're my best friend since Ty Power." Rest in peace; for doth it not come to us all?

Unless one punches out, one *will* be reduced to signing photos at a supermarket opening, shoplifting, reclusion, or self-imitation.

Henry Fonda, than whom we had no finer actor, never received a competitive (real) Oscar till *On Golden Pond*, playing a character part of an old man. I met him on the set of *Summer Solstice*, a Television movie, the ancient template: an old couple reminisces over the oompth decades of their troubled marriage, its early years played by younger actors.

Henry's wife in the film was Myrna Loy, with whom I am still in love. (What more touching and unusual love scene than hers with Clark Gable in *Test Pilot*. His plane runs out of gas and lands in her pasture, she says, "I know you: you're the prince. A nice, charming prince, right out of the sky. A young girl's dream." Check it out.)

I am a devotee of Brazilian Jiu-Jitsu.

I was a high school wrestler and, later, boxed and studied kung fu. But Jiu-Jitsu is the Old Man's Sport: its wisdom is based upon conservation of strength and knowledge of body mechanics.

I've always been built like a mailbox, and from earliest youth was likened to a bear. Having the eye-hand coordination of a sloth, I was happy to find a fighting form that was dependent not on striking (hand or foot quickness and accuracy) but *grappling* (tying up the other guy, and proceeding from there).

I am a pack rat and collect various arcana: aviation memorabilia, Judaica, movie stuff . . . I had the chance to buy a collection of one hundred fifty Film Company Employee Badges some years back. These were not only the majors, but those of the long-forgotten Poverty Row. I didn't meet the reserve bid of five grand and have regretted the loss ever since.

In Martial Arts bumf, I have cartes de visite of two of my favorite actors, both wrestlers: Kola Kwariani, who was in *The Killing*; and Stanislaus Zbyszko, who played, essentially, himself (ex-champion of the world) in *Night and the City* by Jules Dassin (1950).

Other beloved wrestlers included Nat Pendleton (1895–1967). Nat played the cop in *The Thin Man* series, and the cop or the light-heavy in dozens of films. (Light-heavy, a boxing class, here used to denote an actor playing a crook in a comedy.) He was a silver medalist in wrestling at the 1920 Olympics. And everyone said he was robbed.

Mike Mazurki played Moose in the Raymond Chandler film *Farewell My Lovely* (1944). In the '30s he'd been starving as a lawyer and began anew as a professional wrestler before taking his 6'5" to Hollywood.

And I had a photo, signed by Fonda, of him getting sacrifice-thrown by his Jiu-Jitsu instructor. Both in white gis, Henry airborne and looking surprised. Pure gold.*

---

* Orthodox Jews and aviators speak of the past greats as of intimates: the Masters of the Talmud talk about Rashi and Maimonides as close, if momentarily absent, members of the group, just as aviators talk about Ernie Gann or Pancho.

Watching *Kiss of Death*, I see a bulking shape lumbering through the background. It's Dewey Sullivan, who played in Preston Sturges's stock company; and there he is, at the end, not even doing a walk-on but working as an extra.

Thinking about Sturges led me to Veronica Lake.

She plays the angel/waif/love interest in *Sullivan's Travels*, the greatest of American Comedies. For those late to the party, they sculpted her blonde hair in a signature that fell down over one eye. It was so widely copied, women in the Defense Plants began coming to grief at their lathes. So Veronica changed her hairdo.

I saw my first Sturges film in the auditorium at Goddard College in Plainfield, Vermont, in 1973. Later that week some friends and I drove to Burlington.

There was a woman at the diner who caught my attention. On the drive home I said, "Omigod, that was Veronica *Lake*." My friends told me I was just loony-in-love, which I was. What in the world would she have been doing in Burlington? Some years later, reading up on Sturges and his Merry Folk, I learned she'd fetched up in Vermont at a sanatorium. And there she was. And I'd seen her.

Or perhaps not.

Any number of guides, amateur and pro, will take you to the staircase where Laurel and Hardy filmed *The Music Box*, each guide, of course, choosing differently.

In 1973, Veronica went into Burlington Memorial Hospital, where she died of cirrhosis of the liver. Frances Marie Ockelman, that was.

UNTIL. ✒

There I was at some function in the days I thought it good to try to chew the rubber chicken. And, at my table was an attractive older woman. She was introduced, but I didn't catch her name. And as we chatted, I gleaned, from this or that reference, that she was Jane Fonda.

All-that-to-one-side: I was touched by the love with which she described her father. And so, the next morning, I sent her the photo.

See the scene in *Fail Safe*, between Fonda and Larry Hagman. Henry's the president, and Larry's his Russian interpreter, on the phone to the Russian premier. We've just mistakenly dispatched nuclear bombers to Russia.

It's the best scene in The Movies, played against two white walls. *Fail Safe* was directed by Sid Lumet, who directed my script of *The Verdict*. I used to live around the corner from him in Manhattan and had dinner at his house once a month or so. I followed him on the sets of *The Verdict*, and *there* was a lesson. He was so quick we said we were lucky if we got *one* take.

Great lesson. To the contrary, I was on the set of *Wag the Dog*, watching Bob De Niro and Dustin Hoffman shoot a short "talky" scene (God forgive me), and they came into the shot, said the words, and walked out, and, camera still rolling, came in *again*; everyone copacetic with the notion there were many takes required. Problem is that, even were it so (which it isn't), if you can't succinctly tell the actors what you'd like different, you're just burning film or, today, electrons. The problem worsens as you're dumping more film on the editor's desk and exhausting the actors, who, in their uninstructed repetitions, search not for a better way but for a way that might debar them from a) further criticism and b) further pointless effort. This way, inevitably, is "pretending," that is, por-

---

What actual connection could a snakebit fan (myself) (or, for that matter, you) have with Celebrity? Answer, none.

Our babbling praise is, to them, an imposition. Most will be gracious; and many will accept the difficult along with the delightful that comes with their status. And many drink themselves to death.

traying whatever a sentient being might recognize as the approved way to say that line.

Ah, well. Also on the set, I got a hug from Anne Heche, and if she was Gay, she at least during that hug was bisexual.

Pretty swell.

Rest in peace. She died, in a car crash at an intersection just past the departure end of Runway 21, Santa Monica Airport. Some two hundred yards away, on the Penmar Golf Course, Harrison Ford put his broken airplane down in 2016. A superb bit of flying. He'd put the plane, a 1942 Ryan Aeronautical ST3KR, up for sale a year previously, and I'd considered buying it.

A decade ago, the airport was a thriving concern. Harrison kept four or five planes there; and he took me flying in one of them, an Aviat Husky. Tony Bill* took me up in his WACO biplane, and we did lazy eights out over the ocean.

I don't think there is a photo of a pilot and plane in which the pilot isn't smiling. But this smiling was too much for the puritans of the Santa Monica City Council, and the airport's been strangled into nonexistence, and an upcoming new life as a real estate boondoggle.

Most of the back lots of Fox have become Culver City, and the remainder parking for the drones pushing paper and calling it show business. Oh, embittered, embittered Dave.

But my wife, Rebecca, the wisest person I know, is a devoted student of yoga; and her guru is B. K. S. Iyengar, rest in peace. He was asked if he wanted to extend his life, and he said, "Why be greedy?"

Sue Mengers (1932–2011) said, "Show business doesn't owe me a damn thing."

She was the most interesting person in Hollywood. Like Mike Nichols, Francis Lederer, Hedy Lamarr, Billy Wilder, Peter Lorre, and hundreds of others, she was a refugee.

Most, the Jews, as above, fled the Nazis. Alexander Golitzen (1908–2005) fled the Reds. His was one of the richest families in

---

* Producer of *The Sting*, etc.

Tsarist Russia. He got out with the shirt on his back and lived and worked in Hollywood as an art director (*Foreign Correspondent*, *Spartacus*, *To Kill a Mockingbird*).

The Mitteleuropean Jews lived where I live now, in Santa Monica, and down the hill in Rustic Canyon, where the early moguls had their Parcs-aux-Cerfs.*

Santa Monica was known as Weimar on the Pacific. I will note Billy Wilder, coming into a kaffeeklatsch of Hungarians (sign on leaving Metro-Goldwyn-Mayer: It is not enough to be a Hungarian, you must also work), the boys were chatting away in Magyar, and Billy said, "Boys, boys, this is America: Speak German."

Billy and his wife, Audrey, were great friends with my friend Joe Sugarman. Billy died before I washed up out West, but Joe and his wife, Oddy, had us to dinner with Audrey, who told us tales of Old Hollywood. She'd been a singer in Fred Astaire films and said the watchword among the hoofers was "not a word about Fred."†

They were on their second date when Billy asked, "Would you consider leaving show business and marrying me?" And she replied, "I thought you'd never ask."

She can be seen, fleetingly, as the cheating wife quitting the Other Man's bedroom at the Ritz in *Love in the Afternoon*.

This is the perfect Viennese bedroom farce, delivered, by Billy et al., with magnificent reserve. It features Audrey Hepburn; we always said she was Jewish. It turns out she wasn't but Kate Hepburn was. Go figure.

Her love interest is Gary Cooper, who's old enough to be her grandfather. And Billy did it again in *Sabrina*, where Audrey's in love with Bogey, old and ill and tired. God bless him.

But as we age, there ages also our notion of "Young."

---

\* Louis XV's private whorehouse.

† After Billy's death, Audrey gave some mementos to Joe Sugarman. Several years after her death, Joe passed one on to me. It is an African tribal mask, which can be seen behind Billy's desk in many photos. I've tried to hang it here and there but have been unable, to date, to live with it, as it scares the shit out of me.

I'm seventy-five at this writing, and a forty-year-old is a young man.

So Billy, engaging, as all us directors do, in overt or crypto love for his star,* cast a couple of old fellows opposite the world's loveliest young woman.

Audrey was also the sole actress more beautiful than Gary Cooper. (I am tempted to exempt Dietrich in *Morocco*; but I must be true to my girl, just as I would to my School.)

Sue Mengers came over at age six, just ahead of the Nazis. She became not just an agent but a Superagent, representing the Grandes Dames of the seventies (Barbra Streisand, Ali MacGraw, Cher, Candice Bergen, Joan Collins, Faye Dunaway). And she held a salon, to which my wife and I were very pleased to be regularly invited.

Her best friend was Geffen, and she was referred to in the crowd as Mrs. Geffen. He and, I believe, Jack Nicholson bought her her house, behind the Beverly Hills Hotel, and gave it to her when her husband died and she went bust.†

The Beverly Hills Hotel, where I played piano four hands with Randy Newman in the empty ballroom; where Alan King held court in the first booth at the Polo Lounge; where we had burnt Rye Toast and Coffee in the coffee shop served by the same orange-haired waitresses who had served the same for decades and no doubt offered, in their youth, other dainties to the Community.‡

---

* More wisdom from Mike Nichols: it's okay to schtup your Leading Lady. But don't stop. I was always a straight arrow on my sets. First, I *had* a girl; and, then, I was so tired at the end of the shooting day, sixteen hours on my feet. I shot *Heist* with Gene Hackman, then seventy. I was driving him home one night, and he asked me if I ever grew tired on set. I said I did not but that each night when I arrived at my house I had no idea how I was going to make it out of my car.

† Dave and Sue were the best of friends, but one year they had a pseudo-marital tiff and would not hear each other's names. A year passed. David called to bury the hatchet and wanted to get together. The reconciliation as told to me by Sue: "Come by tonight," I said. "There'll be nobody here but no-good, ungrateful faggots." "I'll be there," he said.

‡ Back in the seventies it was not the Industry but the Community that was bicoastal. One would see one's like on Tuesday at Elaine's in Manhattan, then on a

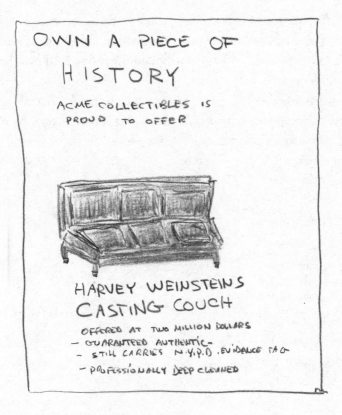

red-eye to L.A., then Saturday morning at brunch at the Bev Hills. These were not the suits but performers and directors and writers, flying back and forth not to "meet" but to work.

The Boeing 747's upper deck was a feature of first-class travel. It was a lounge, a bar. At one time, one of the lines installed a piano. If sleepless or looking for company, one could climb them spiral stairs and find it there.

I saw Alan regularly, not only in his booth at the Bev Hills but in his and Sid's offices in New York. He'd just done *Just Tell Me What You Want*, a Lumet comedy, and we were acquaintances, back when the term meant "friend, adjacent," back before the term meant "friend, former."

Whoopi Goldberg was another of that coterie. Mike Nichols helped put her on Broadway. She and I became friends. I was in the audience regularly. I mention her because of a compliment.

For the question is: What *happened* to those, the prettiest girls in Waxahachie, Walla Walla, Dubuque, who got their on-screen break saying, "One moment please, and I'll connect you . . ." and then were seen no more.

Africans were kidnapped and forced to work American rice fields because a hereditary trait made many of them resistant to malaria, their genetic superiority an unfortunate inducement to their exploitation. See also the casting couch.

---

I was having coffee at Alan's office, and he asked if I'd seen Whoopi's show. "You got to see it," he said. "She *stops* it." He paused. "She stops it *dead*."

From a comic this is the highest praise. One might say "they peed their pants" or "they threw babies from the Balcony," but these phrases are, I think, never uttered about any performance other than one's own, their incipient hyperbole recognizable by all.

But "she stopped the show" is unadulterated tribute.

I mention, also, in this regard, my daughter Zosia. She insisted her way onto the TV show *Girls*.

They wrote her a bit part as Shoshanna, realized their wisdom, expanded the role, and, time after time, she stopped the show.

We may discuss those lauded as "great" (e.g., Laurence Olivier or Gregory Peck) and nod in appreciation. But I explain my relationship to Shoshanna, and folks smile.

# COLLEAGUES AND SWINE

Very little film dialogue is significant. Silent Film stoop-workers included "titles" writers. "Came the Dawn"; "Tahiti: Land of a million memories, awaiting the White Man's Pleasure . . ."; "Bilbergtown, a community of workers, like Doc Miller, and of victims, like Bill Boggs . . ."

None of the silent titles that I've seen would have been missed if excised. Many of them displayed snatches of dialogue from the plays raped onto the screen, but the wiser man might have realized that the titles were showing something that needed no narration ("Mont-Blanc, a looming presence . . .") or that actually impeded the mental processes which moved the audience along. A shot of a drunk at a bar, finishes a glass, and garrulously motions the bartender for another; title: "Jimmy Floyd, the Town Drunk."

Earliest scenarists said they were employed writing "gags and titles," much as a symphony conductor might proudly announce himself a Band Leader. (See Rex Harrison, *Unfaithfully Yours*, 1948.)

Many of the title card writers were women—perhaps a lucky case of proximity to the secretary's typewriter. Many of the women became scenarists, as many of the books adapted to the early screen were written by women, Edna Ferber, Fannie Hurst, Anita Loos, Adela Rogers St. Johns, Vicki Baum, and so on.

Their breakthrough into directing came through the proximity to actual film. (In my day, a long strip, coated with emulsion, run through a mechanical camera, which exposed the 35mm films, twenty-four frames each second. The negative was then boxed and taken to a lab, where it was processed, and a positive print made.)

This positive copy of the original negative (the actual film actually exposed on the set) was cut and assembled by editors. Many of them were women. The women got the job because they were already in the lab, hand-coloring the early silent black-and-white films.

Their hands were smaller than men's, and they were considered more adaptable to the fine work; hand-tinting being the Forbidden Stitch of moviemaking.

Their presence in the lab led to their employment as editors. And there is *no* better way to learn to write or direct a film than editing. Shoot for show, cut for dough.

The editor was doubly blessed (then and now), as she had no investment in the previous work—she hadn't slaved to make the scene work on paper, or spent three months of nights in a sandstorm to film it; she got a load of film dumped on her desk and, with that and the script as a guide, labored to turn it into a movie.

Some women transitioned from the editing room to behind the camera; and many directors (myself among them) learned a bit of craft in the editing room.

I worked for forty years with the great Barbara Tulliver, my friend and "cutter."* She was my pal through many films and TV shows. She saved many a sequence and taught calm and patience. Samuel Clemens was looking at a moon down south, in 1870, and said to a servant, "Look at the moon," and she said, "Lord, Mr. Clemens, you should have seen that moon befoah the Woah." And you should have seen Barbara, a sphinx, sitting calmly while some new assistant hunted for the strip required, upset the rack, spilled coffee, and generally melted down.

On every film, in post-production, I'd get a call, usually late at night, from Barbara, who was still at work. "David, you're going to hate me," which meant she had cut my Favorite Scene, as it was ruining the film.

My friend Ricky Jay died in 2018. He, the greatest magician of his age, was a wonderful actor in the tradition of the other Jewish

---

* Barbara tells me she's taken up writing, having fought clear of the impulse for years until she realized that "writing is just making shit up."

light-heavies, Harold Huber, George Stone, Murray Alper, Paul Stewart, Ricardo Cortez, Abner Biberman, Sheldon Leonard.[*]

See Ricky in *House of Games, Heist, Things Change, Redbelt*, etc. And do treat yourself to this: HBO's *Ricky Jay and His 52 Assistants*, the TV version (directed by me) of his Off-Broadway show.

Ricky had been performing since he was seven. He was the youngest magician ever on TV, on a show called *Time for Pets*. Some of his wisdom: you never know your show till everything that can go wrong has.

Speaking of which, I met with Jim Gandolfini, who'd signed on to a TV pilot I'd written, *The Lake*, about crooks and lawyers (PAUSE) and cops in Chicago.[†]

He said that he adored doing *The Sopranos* and preferred TV to film, as by the time one figured out how to make the film the shooting was over. And he loved the life of the cast and crew, that usually-better-than family.

I, too, loved the camaraderie on my movie sets and was always grateful to be there.

A musician friend told me that she was playing as part of an orchestra backing up A Very Famous Singer, and all the orchestra members had to sign a pledge that they would not look at her.

This is a wrong solution to an actual situation.

Everyone on the set or stage is intent on helping the Director and the Star. Should either of these, when passing through, catch the eye of a crew member (primed to offer assistance), it's incumbent on the person in authority to understand, and not trouble the worker—say hello and move on, *or look down*, but do *not* catch their eye.

Directing a film, in my day, meant taking the helm of a small community of dedicated craftspeople who took pride in fulfilling *any* request. But, note, the request had to be stated in practicable

---

[*] If this ain't a prize instance of film insanity call me a blue-nosed gopher. In the 1946 propaganda film *Little Tokyo, U.S.A.*, Huber, Biberman, and Stone play three Japanese spies.

[†] The project died with Jim, may he rest in peace.

terms. "Could I have a *yellow* one?" Yes. "Can you make it More Inviting?" No.

Nichols said, commuting between the two coasts, that his life in Hollywood was, "What about if the shoes were slingback?" Back in New York, on Broadway, "Why don't we try it upstage of the couch?"

Regarding the crew: when the Director, stumped, is in sad conference with the DP, a crew member might up and say, "This might be stupid, *but* . . ."; and it is *always* wisdom. Recall the truck stuck in a tunnel, this onlooker recommending removing the wheels, that one jackhammering the ceiling, and a young kid stepped up and suggested, "Why not let some air out of the tires?"

I loved hearing from the crew. They were so smart.

Set custom held that one must *never* help another fellow do his job. If you're doing the other guy's job, something is assuredly suffering in your area of responsibility. However—and, indeed, tempered by the universally acknowledged culture of nonintervention—when a department head (sets, lights, gaffers, transportation, costumes, makeup) said, "This may be stupid, *but*" (translation: "I am well aware that I am treading close to a prohibition, and would not do so were I not absolutely sure this will help"), the burden of command was lightened and the clouds of confusion cleared.

Executives have *no* place on the set. They don't know what they're looking at.

Shooting at Oak Street Beach, a resident looked at the infestation of our crew and said, "Don't they have anything better to do? None of them are *doing* anything." While all I saw was ordered activity.

Just as Barbara was the brains of the cutting room, the Assistant Directors were the brains of the set.

I made several films with two greats, Cara Giallanza and Cas Donovan.

As I've said, the Director's job calls for a freak. Directing a film is like playing chess while wrestling.

There I was, for example, between shots (most of the time spent on the set), and I knew I was going to run late—that is, exceed the time allotted per day, by contract, with the crew or cast.

I was going to have to ask the Star—I believe it was Gene Hackman (*Heist*)—to stay five or ten minutes late, for the shot he'd been patiently waiting for.

His contract read twelve hours door-to-door; and if he stayed late, we were going to exceed that and would need his acquiescence. This is no inconsiderable request: the contract should be honored de facto and de jure, as a sign of respect—to transgress its letter or spirit was (and is) the job of the studios and the producers. But the Director (an artist himself) has been on the fuzzy end of the lollipop and may display his respect to his like best by *observance of the contract*.

Now, here's how one directs a film. I am wondering if I can ask Gene to stay late so I can get the shot. He, being a gentleman, will most likely assent—the unspoken agreement, that this is not the new normal but a one-off.

While I am pondering, I am walking the set, which is being dressed (accessorized) for the new scene: lamps, pillows, pictures, tchotchkes, and so on, are being placed on the set by the Set Dressers. They are, professionally, overdressing the set, in order to give me, the Director, choices; I am walking the set, and pointing, "Lose it, lose it, lose it, what happened to the nice dachshund paperweight I saw in the show-and-tell . . . ?" And so on. Simultaneously conferring with the DP (hallowed street name: cameraman) about some aspects of the first shot; and now, if I ask Gene to stay, I am going to squander any opportunity to ask again, should I again come up against it.

I might ask him to stay *if* I can reschedule his early-morning call tomorrow; but it would involve flipping the day's first two scenes. His scene, the first, takes place on a park bench, and his second, on a boat. I don't know if I can have access to the boat first thing, someone will have to call the boat-wrangler. I turn to Cas, and she says, "I've taken care of it."

Cara (I beg pardon if these are twice-told tales) was the AD on *Redbelt*, my martial arts film.

We're shooting the final Big Fight in the Pyramid in Long Beach; the audience is made up of extras and, between them, inflatables, balloons of human torsos dressed appropriately. No one had been asleep for years (the fatigue grows exponentially as one nears the end of shooting, and the surest sign of depletion is the Director's "What do *you* think . . . ?").

We are dead on our feet, and Cara is setting up the next shot, in which the audience has to be moved. She picks up her megaphone and announces, "Alright, now, the Real People, AND THE REAL PEOPLE ONLY . . ."


Good lord we had fun.

And here's a lesson in directing. I wrote and directed *Phil Spector* for HBO Films. I was told, in first negotiations, that they never gave any director final cut. I said that was fine, I'd take my script somewhere else, and they capitulated.

During the cutting process, however, the HBO Executive kept asking to come to the cutting room, with his suggestions.

I eventually tired of reminding him of my contract, and (my mistake) said, alright, come in.

In the cutting room, as on the set, the Director is involved not only with the momentary question but with its ramifications for the entire film. Just as I had to think about Gene Hackman and the boat. In the editing room, a cut might seem appropriate to a well-wisher reflecting solely on the one cut; while the Director knows that this decision is also affected, for example, by a similar cut in the previous sequence not before the outsider.

This Executive didn't know what he was looking at—how could he, as he hadn't lived with the thing as a script, on the set, or through days in the cutting room. He just saw what was in front of him. (He also came forty minutes late to the first screening, but I've forgotten all about it.)

In the cutting room he suggested this or that cut, and I, indictably, sighed, and said, to Barbara, "Yeah, alright, let *him* cut the sequence." He thought a bit and made a suggestion or two; and their awfulness was surpassed by my horror at the realization that I'd just resigned as Director and Barbara, accepting my decision—as was her understanding of her job—was now actually paying attention to this amateur idiot whom *I* had *appointed*. Ashamed (as I am at this writing), I let him conclude his ten minutes of fumbling, ushered him out, with thanks, apologized contritely to Barbara, and asked her to repair the damage I'd caused.

Great are the responsibilities of command and great the pride of having fulfilled them to the satisfaction of the Company. You can't fool the crew.*

I was prepping my script *Blackbird*.

This (never yet made) is a thriller based in Hollywood. The granddaughter of a motion picture effects producer comes to Pasadena on his death, to take possession of the house he left her, and his estate, which has been supplying her and her son with income for some years.

She finds the house was not his, and the money stops. She starts to investigate, and her life is threatened. Great stuff, many surprises.

I, or my terriers, found a French Muslim producer to fund it for a dollar and a half. The reason for my mention of his religion appears a little farther on.

Now, we were very short of funds, and I had already waived my directorial fee and was doing the script for WGA-prescribed minimum. We'd gotten the money, as Cate Blanchett read the thing and said she'd be most happy to play the lead (for minimum).

I flew to Australia to meet her, as did the producer. I found him there (as opposed to in our first meetings in L.A.) cold to me. I asked him why, and he said, "I don't trust you." This was a poser, as I knew of no reason for his distrust; what did he know about me, save that I'd thrown my project into his pot, glad to be making it for the fun of the thing? In any case, there we were. We came back to L.A., where

---

* Are dogs more intelligent than humans? They are certainly more rational, for they do nothing contrary to their own best interest. Playing catch or fetch, the dog can't be distracted by your strategies or body language: they're just watching the ball. The crew, similarly, may notice, but will pay no heed to the moods, impertinence, absurdities, posturing, and ineptitude on the set, they're just there to get it in the can.

I began, in spite of his mistrust, prepping the thing, calling in every favor I could think of.

His pre-production money was not forthcoming, and I'd already reached out to location scouts, with the offer of his promised fee. But their fee wasn't there. I apologized to the location scout I'd chosen and said that I'd cut her a personal check, but she said that was unnecessary, as my word was good enough.

One of my proudest moments as a director.

Well, pre-production went on, everything cut down to the bone. And I realized that we were still several hundred grand away from the barest budget sufficient (God willing) to get the film in the can. I called the producer and asked him to come by my office, and he did so. I told him why we needed the extra cash, and he said he'd have to take it under advisement and would call me back that night. He neglected to call but did, that afternoon, get on a plane to Paris.

I started scrambling, and saw a way through to stitching together the money. I called Cate's agent (Hylda Queally), who said, don't bother, the producer, Saïd Ben Saïd, had already called her and said the film was off, and explained it was my fault, and that I shouldn't be trusted.

Cate thus was correctly being protected by her agent from a failing project, and I can't quite fault the agent for believing the libel. But why did the fellow not trust me?

I paced my office, where we'd first met and discovered, on the coffee table, the first thing he'd have seen on entering, this book: *L'Exil au Maghreb: La Condition Juive Sous l'Islam.*\* Well, I left that book there prior to the inception of the project, but how could he not have considered it a deliberate insult? In effect, he could not. What a shame.

I did enjoy my time in Australia—what little I can remember of it. They do like to drink. Cate was charming.

I spent that year's High Holidays at the Great Synagogue in Syd-

---

\*  Exile in the Maghreb: The Condition of the Jews Under Islam.

ney. I came first on Erev Rosh Hashanah, happy to find the entrance protected by young men and women in combat gear. (America seems to be the sole Western country that does not, as a matter of course, protect its Jewish Institutions.) I was in line to get wanded and frisked when a man came up beside me. "I'm Rabbi X," he said, "and you're David Mamet, coming to our shul. *Welcome.*" "Thank you, Rabbi," I said. The young woman with the carbine said, "Shall we pass him in, Rabbi?" And he said, "Naa, frisk him," which she did.

The movies were never a medium for dispensing justice but rather for selling popcorn.

Who goes out of an evening proposing to be lectured? No one. And now that the cinemas are dying or dead, we stay home, and can, if we wish, skip past the sites flogging racial harmony and national self-hate, and hope to find something worthy, if not of our delight, then at least of our attention.

Marlon Brando sent Princess Sacheen Littlefeather up to accept his Academy Award for *The Godfather.*\* She lectured us about racial injustice to Native Americans. But what did that have to do with him getting a gold star from a bunch of Yids he'd made money for?

And now, each celebrity has his pet disease to be revealed at awards time, the equivalent of the new guest at the dinner table regaling us with the details of his aunt's stomach cancer.

People flourish in hierarchy. Not only those in positions of leadership but those on the shop floor.

---

\* Sacheen Littlefeather, Maria Louise Cruz, was not a Native American. See also the perennial Iron Eyes Cody, designated Indian in countless movies and TV shows, and the iconic image of the "Keep America Beautiful" PSAs of the seventies, in which he shed a tear at the pollution of our national parks. He was Sicilian. Brilliant.

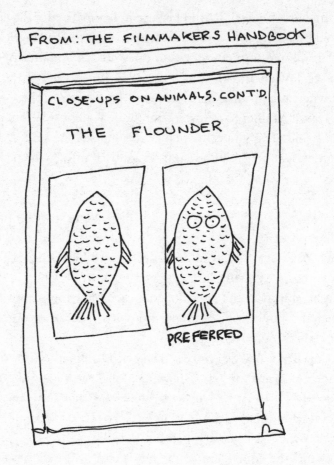

Folks suffer under dictatorship, but everybody craves direction.

Psychotics get it from Mars, the deluded from The Spirits, or The Sunset, the fortunate from Religion or family custom. It's a fine thing to know one's place in an organization whose goals you endorse, when assured that your contribution will be noted and appreciated.

Interchange on a set: Director, myself, needs an immediate alteration in a costume. He calls for the designer, Laura, she's off set, working with her Assistant; and the on-set costume woman is back working in a trailer. Crew looks around, takes in the situation;

and responsibility devolves onto the most proximate responsible person—in this case, perhaps, the set dresser, not a costumer, but also involved in design, who steps up and says, "*I'm* Laura . . ." What a privilege.

See Patrick Dennis, in his *Auntie Mame*. Her wisdom: "Life is a banquet, and most poor sons-of-bitches are starving to death!"

# JUST ONE DAMN THING AFTER ANOTHER

Drama is not the lesson but the *reminder* that nothing in this life is on the level.

We laugh at the machinations of the cheating spouse, the lecher, the politician, the liar—not at the revelation that such exist but at our recognition that "we knew it all along." Of course we did, for we are laughing at ourselves. And at our transparent efforts to keep our motives hidden, not only from others but from ourselves.

We stiffen our necks at the perfidies of the other side's politicos and will hear nothing to the detriment of our own. But a little experience of the world reveals that they're all just politicians, which is to say a bunch of thieves or fools. And we embrace the operations of the thief, fixer, lawyer, or stock manipulator who promises us—as we are wise—the short way to various benefits. We reason that, yes, he is a thug, but how lucky I am that he is *my* thug. Until comes the inevitable dawn.

I've spent fifty years as a dramatist. Not only did it seem the only thing worth doing, it was the only thing I was good at—providing not just joy but self-respect and, after some time, income.

The director and the writer in twentieth-century American theater enjoyed the respect of all—it was awarded not to the holder of office, for his rank, but to one who *held* the office because he could *make it happen*.

"It" was getting the asses into the seats, keeping them there for two hours, and sending them out to tell their friends. The Theater was a meritocracy, for the audience didn't care where one went to school (let alone what race or sex one was), but only if one's work fulfilled the promise of a Good Night Out.

I founded various theaters as a young fellow, and my ability to perform the above attracted co-workers who respected my ability. As I respected theirs.

The Commune (says this child of the sixties) only functions for a short time—till the charisma of its leader becomes tiresome, the vacuity of his vision becomes apparent, or Daddy's loot runs out. Our sprung-from-the-earth theaters of Chicago in the '70s lived through and ended with the success of their members.

For didn't so-and-so go off to New York, or to TV, or to the Movies? Didn't I?

Who doesn't want a raise? The only folk intent on continuing poverty as a badge of election are those with parental or government support. So, any organism's success means *growth*, and growth is the expenditure of strength, the inevitable end of which is decay and death, allowing new growth.

At no point does the healthy, growing organism, having wrested success from an uncaring universe, decide, "I'll play *these*." (See *King Lear*.) The universe will be the judge of that.

My particular road trip took me from Chicago to New York, to Off-Off, Off-, and Broadway, and then, surprise, to Hollywood.

The hegira unfolded in segments.

I've been a writer all my life, delighted every morning to sit down with my cup of tea and a typewriter, and (pick one or both) drive myself crazy or have a swell time.

But New York, may God forgive it, was not ready for two Broadway or Off-Broadway plays a year by the same guy. Yes, yes, Neil Simon, and so on, but, for whatever reason, not me.

And so I wrote for various rags, *Esquire*, *New York* mag, the *New York Times*, the *Wall Street Journal*, *Playboy*, the *Atlantic Monthly*, and so on; and I started writing screenplays.

We know that, given the chance, the bad money will drive out the good, the tail *will* wag the dog; and the tail, in my case, was Hollywood. I began at what I considered the top, as in the foreword. Bob

Rafelson had me ghosting him on the set of *The Postman Always Rings Twice*. "Why, *hell*," I said to myself, of the position of Director, "*I* can do this." As indeed I could, for I'd been doing it for years on the stage.

And I had a good theoretical start, as I'd been given a reading list at the Neighborhood Playhouse.

I spent a year there (1967–68), taught by, among others, Sanford Meisner. I had no idea what he was talking about, but I loved the school library and the reading list books by the early Soviet filmmakers and theoreticians, Eisenstein, Pudovkin, Evreinov.

Their great contribution was the reduction of filmmaking to one simple truth: film is a succession of images *the juxtaposition of which* tells the story to the audience.

See here:

Shot of a man, sitting at a desk, staring off.

His POV: a mantelpiece, an envelope propped up on it.

The man gets up and walks toward the mantelpiece, passing a large window, closed.

Angle, the mantelpiece, the man takes the envelope.

He walks back, taking a letter from the envelope.

Shot of the desk, the man sits, he reads the short letter, he nods, leaves the letter on the desk, and walks out of the shot.

Shot of the window, now open, its drapery blowing in the wind.

Shot of the closed study door. It opens, a young woman enters.

Her POV, the open window.

Her close-up.

Her POV, the desk, papers fluttering in the wind. The letter we saw earlier, held down by a paperweight.

She walks toward the letter.

Shot of her hand, picking the letter up.

That's how, as I learned from the Commies, one writes a film. The audience, like you, the reader, is led, THROUGH A SUCCESSION OF IMAGES JUXTAPOSED, to follow the action, not "understanding," but "wondering" what happens next. So that the end of the sequence is, we very much want to know *what was in the letter—*

which leads us to the *next* sequence, which is logically, what's she going to *do* about it?

This is not a theoretical opinion, it's how we perceive.

The film's act builds on the *sequence* (as above), which is constructed from the most basic element: the shot.

"Yes, but," you might say. What about The Characters?

Best Beloved, there are no characters, there are only actors, and actors are only people.*

The Director is the one person on the set who doesn't have to know anything. The department heads and the craftspeople are magnificently skilled, and have the answer to any question.

But the Director should (and, in the days before identity politics, had to) know *something*—else how to have achieved the position?

He might be good with a camera, or as a designer, or as a writer; and, in my case, my ability as a writer was linked to and *derived from* my work with actors onstage.

For I knew (and it was borne out in practice) that my words were sufficient—they didn't need aid from the actors' embellishments, they only required the actors' courage. This meant stand still, let the words come out clearly, and do not be dismayed by unbidden emotions: they are not engendered by your insufficiency, but *by the script*. Letting them flow unhindered is what we see in that acting we call genius.

That's what I brought to film directing: the knowledge that the actor didn't need to help it, and that the audience would be grateful for the omission. We all know this, as we get up to leave the room when the television devolves to the Narrative Scene. And we of the Profession may learn it, when even prior to the influence of our paycheck, our self-respect depends on it.

---

* Who were the "characters" in the above sequence? What did you know about them? Nothing. What did you miss?

When you've got the paying customers out front and they nod off during your beloved keystone scene, you carry that humiliation to the grave. And when your livelihood depends on it, you make *sure* you don't do it no more. (Exceptions were, and are, the state-supported Theater, living on the subsidy of your tax dollars or the charity of subscribers willing to be bored spitless for a good cause.)

So I went, bit by bit, much like a Missionary among cannibals who had refrigeration. Bit by bit, to Hollywood.

And no one out there, in forty years, liked my scripts.

I exempt five directors,* the actors, and the audience.

I came to Hollywood, as all news comes, from the East; I was a novelty, and a success; and most business arrangements started with, "I so respect your work, I love everything you've ever written," and ended with, "except *this*."

Time and again, and *to this very day*, I've been baffled by the inability of producers, studio executives, managers, and agents to read a script.

Or, better, to read a script written as direction to the director and cinematographer in order to complete a film that would, through the precision of its construction, enthrall, delight, amuse, or shock a paying audience.

Who were these fools? The wiser ones, the old moguls, and independent producers, were happy to be hustling for millions, rather than on the street corner, asking, "Wanna buy a watch?" I understood these guys, for was I not one of them? The difference between us was this: after the deluge, I figured I could probably get dinner by telling a tale at the Campfire; but Civilization would have to, once

---

* Bob Rafelson, Sid Lumet, John Frankenheimer, and Danny DeVito. I never worked with the fifth, but he paid me the highest compliment. In 1992, Volker Schlöndorff made a documentary about Billy Wilder. He asked about the paucity of good scripts, and Billy replied, "Not everyone can be a Mamet."

again, crawl its way back, before their like would emerge to say, "Kid, I think I can book you at a better campfire."

Now, all things, in my senescence, have, of course, gotten worse. No one in Hollywood today matures in the experience of seeing something with his name on it fail in front of that audience which is paying the rent. But to return to the Neighborhood Playhouse, Stanislavski's books were on the list. His *An Actor Prepares* and *Building a Character* were a bunch of drivel, leading not only to the self-absorption of James Dean but to the beatification of Brando. And to the sustenance of seventy years' worth of so-called teachers of acting.

But Stanislavski's autobiography, *My Life in Art*, is a thrilling read. The tale of his founding of the Moscow Art Theatre was not only an inspiration for me, and Billy Macy, Steven Schachter, and Patty Cox, in creating the St. Nicholas Theatre in Chicago (1973), but a storehouse of practical shop-floor hints.

He wrote that the director should learn shorthand, in order to keep notes at the pace of the actors in rehearsal; and he suggested the director learn to draw.

I never took to shorthand, and I never learned to draw. But I did learn to sketch.

This was of *some* help in the Theater. Not much, because the sets were worked out with designers who could draw; and the position of the actors could *only* be worked out in rehearsal.

Stage directors have, famously, been pictured moving cardboard figures around a scale model of the set. But a play's actual blocking depends not on a *picture* but on the changing relationship between the actors and its correct communication to the audience.

There's a palpable electricity between actors onstage. Left alone, they will usually arrange themselves, beat by beat, in order to achieve that position best calculated to achieve their ends. Just like prize-fighters. And these positions will communicate this changing relationship to the *audience*.

Sketching was of little use to me as a stage director; but for the film director it is all in all.

For, as in the example at the head, the good film is a succession of shots; and each shot can be reduced to a simple sketch.

Most directors, in my days in Hollywood, and, it seems, all today in the Age of Dismemberment, consider moviemaking the capture of action. Generally, the record of: violence or sex—these incidents separated by narration. The audience doesn't care about the narration (and neither do the filmmakers), but it is included as the final homage vice pays to virtue—separating the films by that thin membrane between moviemaking and outright pornography, or Grand Guignol.

But on *my* hill, filmmaking was a) the construction of a plot that could be recorded, shot by shot, and cut together to tell a story (as per the script); and b) the camera's record of *those shots* made on a location or set.

The great director's tool is the storyboard. This is a panel-by-panel cartoon of the script, made in conjunction with the storyboard artist. The cut film should be the direct rendition of the storyboard. (What else could it be?)

Most contemporary directors proceed from "an idea" to the shot list. This is the plan of operations, issued each day, to the crew, and lays out that day's work.

1. Marge enters. Master, Marge and Sheila.
2. Medium shot, Marge and Sheila.
3. Close-up, Marge.
4. Close-up, Sheila . . . etc.

It can be observed that most films are today shot thusly. Which is why they are all the same. But I took real satisfaction from figuring out a sequence shot by shot. A day of planning in which I had one good idea was, for me, a great day. And when I'd reduced the film to the storyboard, and the shot list *from* it, I could walk on the set and shoot it.

I didn't have to "feel" anything, neither did the actors. Neither they nor I had to "carry the film"; they had, as per the script, merely to "walk in the room" or "shoot the intruder," as the case may be, saying the words thoughtfully supplied to them.

This mechanical method took the anxiety out of filmmaking, for no one was asked to do something either unclear or stupid. And so all my sets were happy. Why not? People scream on sets because they are frightened, and they are frightened because they don't know what to do, the clock is ticking, and everyone is watching.

I was on the set of *Things Change* with my friend Shel Silverstein. He saw me sketching Don Ameche and said I should do cartoons. I told him I couldn't draw, and he said, "Neither could Thurber." And here we are.

# A DINOSAUR

My friend Noma Copley (1916–2006) led an interesting life. During the war she was a translator on Eisenhower's staff in France. She was responsible for discovering Cartier-Bresson, engaging him to document the atrocities of the camps.

She was great friends with Magritte and Man Ray and can be seen in many of Man's photographs. We have one, in which she's displaying her hands and, on them, jewelry of her design.

After the war she worked for Walt Disney. She told us that, when she was hired, she was asked into his inner office, the walls of which depicted Disney characters involved in an orgy. "Call me Walt," he said. "Yes, Mr. Disney," she replied.

We had dinner recently with Rebecca's cousin Paul Huson. He was a child actor in films, playing with Larry Olivier in *Richard III*. His mother, Olga Lehmann, whom I knew, was a painter and designer. After the war she worked for Elstree Studios, designing clothes and sets, and painting those portraits of the stars that appeared on-screen.

I told Paul I'd just read that Olga had worked for Errol Flynn, designing his Caribbean hotel. Yes, he said, and she covered the dining room in a mural depicting him in various swashbuckling guises. The mural was done on canvas, and removed before the hotel burnt. But no one knows where the mural is. Nor if there are photos of Mr. Disney's studio *ornée*. Nor if the story is true.

But I drank now and then with Roland Winters, famed for playing Charlie Chan. He was an old and longtime member of The Players club, I was a new light, come for the bar and the poker (Wednesday afternoons, and Saturdays).

Roland stayed in the bar playing gin, but I was up in the library at the poker table. And there, every week, was Eddie Bracken, comic genius of Preston Sturges's *Hail the Conquering Hero* and *The Miracle of Morgan's Creek*. The game was always seven-card stud. Eddie had "The Bracken Theory," that if an opponent held four open cards of a suit, he didn't have a fifth in the hole, and so it was safe to call.

He was a rotten poker player, as was Walter Matthau. I played with him in the famed Begelman Game in Century City.* Matthau came late to the poker game and announced he'd picked five out of seven winners at Hialeah. I knew without asking that, although he'd picked them, he had not bet. And that proved to be the case. He'd penciled in the winners at home, and came to the game, happy with his non-remunerative prescience, to lose at poker. I lost that night, too; playing at a table far over my head, and happy to get away cheaply.

Roland often told the story of John Barrymore at The Players. Barrymore had been barred for showing up drunk, drinking on, and sweeping the glasses and bottles from the bar with his cane. On his reinstatement a member standing at the bar, and just returned from overseas, asked, "Jack, why'd they kick you out?" Barrymore said, "For doing *this*," and took his cane and swept the top of the bar clean.

I met Neil Fitzgerald at the club. He'd been a member of the Abbey, and played for John Ford in *The Informer*. He was friendly with Margaret Hamilton, the Wicked Witch of the West, who lived just kitty-corner from the club around the park.

Neil invited me to go with him to her Christmas Party, but I didn't go. And I didn't go to meet Brando when he and I were both

---

* For latecomers, David Begelman became head of Columbia Pictures in 1973. In '77 Cliff Robertson discovered that Begelman had been forging his name on checks. Cliff blew the whistle. The cops uncovered extensive Begelman forgery and he was eventually ousted from Columbia. The *Wall Street Journal* exposé got turned into the bestseller *Indecent Exposure* (1982). Cliff Robertson got graylisted for talking out of school, and Begelman blew his brains out in 1995.

shooting in Montreal—but I treasure Jack Nicholson's stories of him.

Jack lived up on Mulholland, and Marlon had the neighboring estate. According to Jack, no door could defeat Marlon if he got the munchies and found his cupboard bare; so Jack had to wreath his refrigerator with thick padlocks and chains.

Neil Fitzgerald told me that he was the man who killed Otis Skinner. Neil was onstage, on Broadway, in 1941 in *Mr. Wookey*. Mr. Wookey and his brood live through the Blitz. At one point a buzz bomb is heard, and a young Wookey (Fitzgerald) screams, "*LOOK OUT!*" As he does so he sees an ancient fellow in the front row clutch his chest. He said that's how he killed Otis Skinner.

Otis's daughter, Cornelia Otis Skinner, traveled through Europe with her great chum Emily Kimbrough. The two of 'em wrote of their 1920 Wanderjahr in *Our Hearts Were Young and Gay*. It was adapted as a film, a stage play, a musical comedy, and a short-lived TV series. (Note from Wikipedia: during WWII German intelligence used it for a codebook.)

Emily's niece, Linda Kimbrough, was a colleague in our Chicago theater companies. She can be seen in my film *Spartan*, as the Secret Service agent, and in *State and Main*, my film location comedy, as Edith Head.

Olga worked for Charlie Chaplin on *Monsieur Verdoux*.

Charles Bronson lived in Malibu and painted extensively under his birth name, Buchinsky. I've always felt I'll discover one of his paintings at the Santa Monica flea market.

Nobody knows who knows what happened to the ebony dildo incised in silver with his name which was used to kill Ramon Novarro. Nor has authenticated the original Maltese Falcon. Nor identified the killers of Ron and Nicole.

In 1870 Heinrich Schliemann unearthed the ruins of Troy, a city whose existence, prior to his discovery, was considered a myth.

Paleontologists assert they can re-create a dinosaur based upon discovery of one bone, but where is the creature, long dead, come back to explain "it wasn't that way at all."

And then hear his report ridiculed?

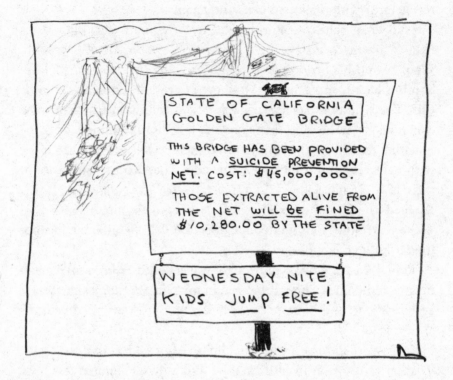

# TOOLS

Writing with a fountain pen employs a physical action and rhythm different from typing. How can the change be without effect?

I do most of my writing on a typewriter. The current page is in the machine; the stack of blank paper is to my left, and the just-typed page to my right. When I finish typing a page, I place it, faceup, upon the pile to my right; and, so, am looking at the typewriter page and its predecessor at the same time. One page is in my hand, another is before my eyes, and I am continually engaged (consciously or not) in the piece's *development*.

When one finishes typing a computer page, it goes away. The new technology, to a debatable but inevitable extent, must influence composition.

There was no greater or more versatile American director than Howard Hawks: *Scarface, Only Angels Have Wings, His Girl Friday, The Big Sleep.* In 1955 he directed *Land of the Pharaohs*, the worst piece of trash ever perpetrated. What happened? CinemaScope.

It was Hawks's first CinemaScope picture. 'Scope doubled the height-to-width ratio of the screen. It was the New Toy 'neath the filmmakers' Xmas tree; but even the best (Hawks), thrilled at the new possibilities, were baffled by its demands. They were like the stage director enlisted to create pageants. Even when Hollywood made good movies, they never could enthrall us at the Oscars. The Oscars were, essentially, the halftime pageant. Ten Dallas Cowgirls were cute, ran their reasoning, so, as one had to fill the field, wouldn't five hundred be cuter?

*Land of the Pharaohs*, produced and directed by one of the greatest of storytellers, begins with hours of Egyptians Marching in Triumphant Procession. In "real life" one would take the gas pipe rather than look out the window to see such a sight, but there Hawks was, his talent unseated by the *requirements* of the new toy.

He went to Egypt (or Spain, or Fresno, or wherever he shot it), and what did he find there? Sand.

Sand is not interesting. Ah, but he was telling a story of the construction of those Necro-McMansions of Old in the sand. *That* might be interesting. And indeed it might, but rather than thinking about holding the audience's interest through the unfolding of *that* story, he was chained to the requirements of a tool.

It cost a mint to go to Egypt. Once there, one would not say, "I have to make the sand interesting,"* but "Let's begin with a sequence of *showing* how powerful Pharaoh was." How? We'll show how many legions of soldiers and slaves he had. How? We'll hire them, and *film* them. Endlessly. Walking on the sand. Lots of them. Like limitless Dallas Cowgirls.

The enormous cost of early CinemaScope would not have been justified by staying in North Hollywood to remake *The Maltese Falcon*. The outlay could only make sense for the photography of Sweeping Natural Majesty. But sweeping natural majesty, though it might do for a travelogue, has *no place in drama*. If Barbara has just discovered her spouse is cheating on her, she is not paying attention to the stark grandeur of the adjacent Atlantic Shore.

Early 'Scope was exploited to film landscapes (or, as the old film quip had it, a snake or a train). Attention given to the squeaky wheel (the location, and the creation of crowd scenes to fill it) was not and *could* not be given to the plot.

Further, early 'Scope (*Land of*, etc.) filmed close-ups by sticking the actor dead center in the middle of the screen. As if his portrait were painted in the middle of the dining room table. Both leaving a lot of dead space on either side.

We are all seducible by novelty. Aren't we spending our waking

---

* Although that is what one meant.

hours "just having to check *this* . . ."? The CinemaScope technology was so dazzling that Hawks didn't stop to evaluate it. He might have done so by asking how CinemaScope could have been used to better *Scarface*. (Answer: It could not.)

Hawks was crippled not only by the machine but by his hats. He was wearing two of 'em. It's the director's job to muscle from the producer as much budget and distance as he can. Hawks was both director and *producer*. Who do you like in a fair fight?

The film credits three writers, one of whom was William Faulkner. I don't know how Faulkner would have spoken at lunch, but I suspect his two Jewish Teammates* were all about "This'll kill 'em . . ." But it did not. The technology killed the movie, as where our Purse is, there our Heart shall be.


The Committee is a tool in movies as in government, devouring the greatest share of the organization's resources. It might seem to exist as a Counsel of the Wise, but it is actually a mechanism for the apportionment of blame.

The factor common to bad Studio-era films and our current drivel seems, obviously, to be fear. Less obviously, but perhaps more usefully, it may be said to be the Committee.

Progenitors and the founders die off, but their vision and accomplishments live on, discernible in the dead husks of the bureaucracies their success engendered.

But the Committee, like kudzu and houseguests, will not die. It attracts ever more adherents possessing no distinction other than devotion to membership-at-any-cost. It carries and transmits the age-old immutable lessons of bureaucratic survival. It will name them anew in each new generation, of course, just as all toothpaste is labeled new and improved.

All toothpaste is some variation on baking soda and mint. One

---

* Harry Kurnitz and Harold Jack Bloom.

can as effectively brush the teeth with salt. The fortunes spent on its constant, insistent rebranding as New must indicate that it's unchanged.

It's the dramatist's job to call attention to the screamingly obvious. Why has it avoided scrutiny? Because it has been repressed. It would not require the enormous energy of repression *unless* it were screamingly obvious. The repression thus is a diagnostic tool.

The formation of the Committee, like most human behavior, is an autonomic production of the sympathetic nervous system or some such thing. The Committee springs to life, and, that life being human, strives to explain to itself why it is here. The urge to share responsibility, and the fear of both error and censure, are inevitable and ineradicable components of communal life. So far, so good, but fear makes wretched storytellers.

# DESTROYED BY TOBACCO

Old-timers tell the new pro boxers they're going to get their head shook, their money took, and their name in the undertaker's book.

Marines inform recruits they'll get screwed, blued, and tattooed.

The prediction, in my racket, is expressed as "Welcome to Hollywood."

But *somebody* killed Marilyn, and William Desmond Taylor, and the wives of various screen notables (Robert Blake, R. J. Wagner, O. J. Simpson). And somebody framed Fatty Arbuckle, and graylisted Cliff Robertson; and many threw their friends under the bus of Joe McCarthy; and many do the same today of this or that person accused of not only crimes and misdemeanors but violation of some newly evolving taboo.

And life on set is *physically* dangerous. There are pyrotechnics, firearms, vehicles moving, a ticking clock, mounting fatigue, and often incomprehensible or absurd directions from on high. And life on the set is the *escape* from the pointless absurdity of Corporate Loathsomeness.

Frederick Law Olmsted (1822–1903), remembered as the architect of Central Park, also directed the United States Sanitary Commission, created to deal with invalids and veterans during the Civil War. He was a farmer, a surveyor, a sailor, and a traveler. I recommend to you his *A Journey in the Seaboard Slave States*, 1853–54.

He was a Yankee, a Christian, and an abolitionist, but he writes not as an advocate but as an economist. That slavery was an unutterable evil is evident not in his commentary but in his reportage.

Virginia, with soil, climate, water transport, and natural resources superior to those of the rich Northern states, he writes, was none-theless poor. The soil was exhausted by the constant replanting of tobacco; manufacture was nil, the simplest of implements were imported from the North, waterpower was not exploited, and the populace was indolent.

He attributes their decay in the midst of abundance to a cultural derogation of labor—that is, of the relationship between cause (work) and effect (prosperity).

The Cavaliers, who were Virginia's Planter Class, considered themselves Lords, which arrogance was, of course, aided by their exploitation of slaves.

The slaves not only did the fieldwork but were the artisans. They were the weavers, millers, blacksmiths, mechanics, tailors, carpenters; their wages kept by their owners.

But as the slaves were not working for themselves, they did not, as may be imagined, work with the same zeal that inspired Northern laborers. The slaves were supported—at a subsistence level, but nonetheless—independent of their work's quality or quantity.

And so the cost of that produced by slave labor, as Olmsted demonstrates, was four times higher than that of free—and had they paid for labor, and that labor's income been tied, as per usual, to production, the resultant profit would have compensated the South for the emancipation of their slaves.

The destruction of the Biz by Diversity Commissars is not the cause, but a result, of corporate degeneracy. The hegemons, as they grow fat, become less sassy, and the confusion about *objective* (making money by supplying a need) caused by affluence attracts exploiters as the sun calls forth maggots from a dead dog.

The DEI (diversity, equity, and inclusion) apparatchiks are one with the life coaches, therapists, and personal shoppers of Beverly Hills—they are the outsourcing of commercial reason by those who can't be bothered.

To get serious for a moment: the appropriate Los Angeles political entities don't need to "solve the Homeless Problem"; they simply need to do what they were hired for: to enforce the laws pertaining to Homelessness. Should that enforcement cause the Homeless to go elsewhere, the City Council, etc., will have done its job.*

* Just so, the purveyors of Hollywood Product, Public Companies, haven't been so placed to solve (real, imagined, or exploited) social problems but to entertain a paying audience.

"Ignorance is weakness; and the ignorant man instinctively merges his ambition and his claims of justice with those of an aggregate—makes that aggregate an object of partiality and bigotry, and finds satisfaction for his enthusiasm in the success of those who guide and represent it, though that success in no wise affect his own interest," Frederick Law Olmsted, *A Journey in the Seaboard Slave States.*

---

# THE TRAUMA IN THE BOATHOUSE

Screenwriting is mechanics. The producers, if they read a script at all, look at the dialogue, and skip over what they (erroneously) call the Stage Directions.

The term is an error, as Stage Directions, in their correct home (the theater), describe what *the actor does*, and the various gags the designers may have whipped up ("she sits in the wing chair," "a window breaks").

The descriptions in a (useful) filmscript relate what the *camera* does. If the shots are correctly described and engineered into a captivating progression, it makes no difference what the actor says. (Watch a film with the sound off, and you'll see.)

The dialogue is of as little concern to a skilled screenwriter as auto paint is to the mechanic. When the machine is correctly assembled, the thing can be painted whatever damn color pleases the money guy. In fact, the money guy *himself* can choose the paint and slop it on, awarding himself the name of co-creator.

That the screenwriter is a mechanic is not poetry. The skilled scenarist is given an idea or a book to adapt (a load of crap). He must first determine the form: a comedy, a light comedy, a comedy of manners, a tragedy, a thriller, tearjerker, noir, drama. He then asks, "How does it function," or "Who does what to whom, and *then* what happens?" He then must find the limits of the machine's operation: How (why) does it begin? What is the event that brings the thing into being? In *Bad Day at Black Rock*, the bad Westerners kill a returned Nisei serviceman, and Spencer Tracy gets off the train to avenge his friend. In *The Russians Are Coming the Russians Are*

*Coming*, a Soviet sub, in the midst of the Cold War, grounds on Nantucket Island, and the sailors must get away unnoticed.

And so on. Without this determination we have the Present Participle Films, the ongoing situation, waiting, being, getting (exception: *Being There*): the form so beloved by the French.* The end of the effective piece must be the solution of the problem caused by the beginning. This seems fatuous, but consider how unfortunately often the mechanical verity is overlooked.

Psychological Dramas avoid mechanical connection between cause and effect through Wish Fulfillment. Here, as in the Analyst's office, the Shrink, through sitting in the dark and (one would hope) listening, finds the "Magic Ticket" in the patient's monologue, brings it to the sap's attention, and all is well. The audience, similarly, is cured and released by the all-powerful words "The End."

But if the solution were that simple and obvious, the problem could not have been that pressing, could it? As Mr. Meisner said, "The Ouch must be related to the Pinch."

The magical awakening with which the movie-as-shrink brings the neurotic (viewer) to health is exactly that of the kiss with which the Handsome Prince wakes Sleeping Beauty. It indicates we were watching a fairy tale. There's nothing wrong with fairy tales, but their construction is of small interest to the artisan who delights in sussing out the *mechanical* cause and effect of human interactions.

Adolescent Achievement Dramas employ the same tools of supernormal intercession (*The Bad News Bears*, *Fame*, etc.). In *School of Rock*, the doofus, anti-talented high school musicians become stone-cold genius rockers when they "just get the idea." Just as the neurotics (on-screen or on the couch, perhaps) are supposedly cured

---

* And by various writers and their adherents among academics and critics insensible to talent. All high school students once were forced to read *The Great Gatsby*. What was Scott Fitzgerald's particular and ongoing problem? He wanted to be liked by rich people. He wasn't fit to puke into the same toilet as Hemingway, whose genius has always been dismissed by dead spirits as "too."

of their compulsion to X when the shrink helps them to recall "what happened that time in the boathouse."

The ignorant producer's eye goes to a narration, in the script, of that boathouse desecration (porn). But to the mechanic screenwriter, not only could it not matter less, it is actually an impediment to the script's operation.

I'll prove it to you.

Young Francesca has for much of her life been horribly addicted to senseless acts. The Wise Psychiatrist brings the sufferer to a recollection of THAT REPRESSION WHICH HAS CAUSED ALL THE BOTHER.

We see the poor thing on the couch as her eyes grow wide, tears start to flow, and she turns, hesitant, wonderingly, to the Doctor. "Omigod," she says, "*I remember now!*" She leans in toward the doctor and tells him the secret, whispering.

We don't hear it.

Wait.

Now she is walking out of the office building, smiling, and into the arms of that Significant faithful Otter who has put up with all the bullshit as he knows her essential goodness.

But we never heard the *story* . . .

What have we lost?

We waited for the confession of "that time in the boathouse," and we didn't get it. So what? For, note, it was just salaciousness, invented to explain otherwise incomprehensible (nondramatic) behavior.

This confession is the noted "death of my kitten" speech, coming midway through the last act, and taking up the slack the dud screenwriter inserted *faute de mieux*.

That we weren't privileged to hear the confession entails on us a sort of Hippocratic Oath, as, one might hope, it does on a real psychiatrist. It enlists us in the Service of *Reserve*.

We are actually ennobled by the frustration of our curiosity, taking away from the film not the sick thrill of another's dirty laundry but relief at the Hero's release. The whispering puts us in the same boat as the protagonist, which is the actual job of the writer-engineer.

If the handsome prince is described as a tall, hefty Black man, and the description does not happen to be our own, we are taken out of the story. Which is why, in fairy tales, he is only described as a Handsome Prince (with thanks to Bruno Bettelheim).

If the protagonist confessed the horrors he or she underwent that time at the office party, we may enjoy the gossip, but unless we personally have undergone a similar horror, the story is no longer about ourselves; if, however, the patient *whispers*, it is. For we experience not the (confected) quiddities of the outrage but community with the sufferer, who, like us, has undergone trauma.[*]

In film the inspired music teacher and the psychoanalyst are, essentially, faith healers, preaching that "belief"; and confession will force the Superior Entity (in the religious story, known as God) to cough up the scarlet ribbons.

But the engineer can only work on a mechanical contrivance, which will not respond to wishing, new paint, or anything less than a technical understanding of the machine's operation.

The craftsman looks at the script (or, indeed, creates one), asking: How is this scene the necessary preamble to the following? If this scene were removed, would the audience still follow the story? If the answer is yes, it must be removed, as the craftsman knows that if it is not, the audience's attention will not wait but will falter.

One must ask, throughout, if the pinch and ouch are connected, or if they are merely contrivances (fig leaves) allowing one to write yet another meaningful scene. ("Jimmy, I thought I loved her, but she said *ex cetera*, and so I have to call the engagement off . . .")

If the extra scene must go, must not the extra line go also? Yes. The producer plumps for exposition, as that is all he read (if he read anything), but the audience doesn't care.

My proof concludes.

---

[*] The film confession, on the other hand, rewards our acceptance of dramatic ineptitude with permitted voyeurism. The trick is widely employed by showing an on-screen funeral.

The reader may still be disturbed or unconvinced by my suggestion of the protagonist's whispering. What would he have remembered had I actually written the obligatory confession? What does he remember of *any* of those speeches that he's heard in films? But you remembered the whispering.

# LIME ROCK

I took a Formula 1–ish driving course. The instructor's opening remarks: "There are two things you can't tell an American man he doesn't know how to do. One of them is drive a car."

But there is a third thing, and it is "write."

No fooling, this calls up as much rage as the other two.

I know it's true of me, as you will have seen in these essays. And it's true of you.

From the time we cry, we make sounds to influence those around us. With the exception of exclamations of joy, hurt, or surprise, this is, in fact, the sole reason anyone makes these sounds.

And we all love to tell stories. They, after all, are one means— their other excellences aside—for immobilizing a group (audience or dinner party). That is, for exercising power.

Bores are practicing a long-perfected skill. The bore can keep an audience as surely as a good raconteur, and more certainly than a poor one.

I turn now to advice given gratis, and recall, to readers, the words of A. E. Housman:

When I was one-and-twenty
    I heard a wise man say,
"Give crowns and pounds and guineas
    But not your heart away."

He is, of course, talking of the Tender Passion, where, we know, it is true. But it's even truer of Free Advice on writing.

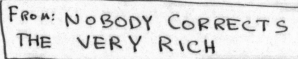

This one or that would send me scripts, either to admire or with hope I could advise them. It was easy to gauge them—three or four lines would reveal whether the chap could write or not. How many bites of fish does one need to determine it's tainted?

I could then, with a clear conscience, write back that I loved it. This was all most wanted, and I was free and clear. Some, having snared *their* fish (me), would respond, then, why not pass it along to your agent or producer?

Le Carré writes of his master spy, Smiley, that he had spent his life in deception but still didn't know how to get out of an unwanted dinner invitation. Who does?

Asked to "pass the thing along," and tired of the natural result of my prevarication (aren't we all), I would have to improvise the "They aren't taking on any new clients," or "The producer is retired, and I *myself* can't get my newest work placed." And so on, self-maneuvered into a certainly transparent falsity; this, at least, putting me on the same degraded level as the plaintiff.

How to avoid the (self-imposed or not) impositions?

First, to explain that my lawyer advised me that I could not expose myself to their efforts, lest someone somehow publish, stage, or film something in which the supplicant might recognize (wrongly, but arguably) something of the work submitted to me.

Why, no (however), he might say, under no circumstances would I traduce my respect for you by suggesting such a thing.

And here is the genius riposte: Of course not, I would say; but, should you, may God forbid, die, and your *heirs* stage, publish, or film your work, OR should you sell it to another producer, and he, doing the same, perceive the similarity in a work of mine and compare the copyright dates (the other fellow's work being registered first), *that* litigious bastard might sue me or my heirs for plagiarism.

This is, of course, the very long way around the barn. I liked it for its suggestion, to the applicant, of the eventual production of his work. Perhaps I liked it more than they did; but in the exchange, as I was not dismissing but endorsing the work's worth, my listener was not called upon to defend his creation (whether or not I was a superior); and might, thus, accept my demurrer without danger to his self-esteem.

Yeah yeah yeah.


I got thrown out of Williams Sonoma for the following:

I'd entered by a parking lot door marked NO ADMITTANCE, PLEASE GO TO THE FRONT ENTRANCE.

A young employee called my attention to my gaffe. I said, "It's alright, I'm an Illegal Immigrant."

She said she found that deeply offensive, and I was escorted out.

Okay. It was not farting in church, she and I each had the joy of our umbrage, but I didn't get my wife's requested Jordan Almonds.

And this got me thrown out of USC film school.

I was invited to talk to some class about Dramatic Writing. One student asked, "What's the best thing I can do to increase my chances of writing for television?"

I considered dissuading him with the end of the Housman poem:

When I was one-and-twenty
    I heard him say again,
"The heart out of the bosom
    Was never given in vain;
'Tis paid with sighs a plenty
    And sold for endless rue."
And I am two-and-twenty,
    And oh, 'tis true, 'tis true.

I thought better of it and replied, "Cut off your dick and eat it."

# TEMPER AND GAGS

I never lost my temper on the set. Why would I? I was thrilled to be there, and I knew there was one person in charge of making sure everyone was happy and productive, and that person was me. But if I *had* lost my temper, it would have been during pre-production of *House of Games* (1987).

We were in Seattle, then a poor and decaying, lovely city. I'd had a dream. In this dream a horse was running at the local track, Long-acres, the next day, and it had something to do with the movies.

I woke, and found, in the morning paper, Scriptgirl, running in the fifth, going off at 17-to-1. I gave my assistant, Scott Zigler, a thousand dollars, and told him to put it on the nose, on Scriptgirl.

End of the day, and I heard on the radio that Scriptgirl had won and, from Scott, that he forgot to go to the track.

Bob Rafelson was shooting *Black Widow* in Seattle. He asked me to play a cop in one scene, and I went over, on my lunch hour, to play the part. Debra Winger was starring, and running a high-stakes blackjack game for herself and the teamsters. Scott and I won several thousand dollars, which lessened the pain. And Scott (with whom I worked often) directed my *The Old Neighborhood* on Broadway in 1997 and many of my plays in New York and elsewhere. But on *House of Games* he was new to the Biz, and so the butt of that concomitant of filming: gags. Film motto: Gags first. Filming, time permitting.

I don't know how (or why) a contemporary crew would get along without gags. For if life on the set is not amusing (in addition to and offset by being exasperating and draining), one's in the wrong business.

It's always been the lower-class kids who are the boxers. If you're not prepared to take a beating in order to succeed, you don't belong in the ring—the beatings you take inspire you to stop taking them and learn to administer them. One can't enter boxing horizontally, through "boxing school."

The folks in my day, in the movies, had to fight their way in. All were proud, the departments, the actors, their pride expressed in an esprit de corps, a large part of which expression was gags.

Scott was in charge of our Establishing Shot. Executives adore the establishing shot. I was doing my TV show *The Unit*, and the suits demanded an establishing shot of the Capitol to convince the audience that they were actually seeing something in Washington, D.C. They *then* demanded we super, over the shot, the legend WASH-INGTON, D.C. For the benefit of whom?

Why, of their rice bowls, of course. For if they weren't dreaming up nonsense, what were they *doing* there? We had Monday morning read-throughs of *The Unit*, infested with various barnacles from The Studio. I asked one what his particular job was, and he replied, "Facial hair."

So Orion, the producers of *House of Games*, demanded an opening, establishing shot of Seattle. I told them, "Why?" Pause. "It's not important that it's Seattle," I said. "Those who wouldn't recognize Seattle aren't going to know anything more than that it's a city. And the residents will no doubt recognize their hometown." No. They demanded the shot.

So I had Scott arrange it. He put a large mirror faceup on a large table and behind it put a poster of Seattle Harbor, or whatever it's called. He then bought a child's tiny, flat-bottomed pull toy of a tug-boat, attached a string, and pulled it slowly across the mirror, for the shot. During which, we sprinkled water from a watering can onto the construction, ending the shot with the watering can becoming visible.

We sent the shot with the dailies to Orion and never heard back. The shot wasn't included in the film, but I count it my finest hour.

Balanced by the below.

*House of Games* was a hell of a film. Orion wouldn't promote it—why should they, as they'd already gotten their money (four million) back in Foreign Sales—but Roger Ebert, then the country's most important film critic, called it "The Year's Best Film."

And then I was shooting my next film, *Things Change*, in Tahoe, and got a call from the head of a Very Important European Film Festival. He told me *House of Games* was to be awarded the festival's highest prize and looked forward to seeing me the next week to accept it.

I said, wait, the Judges haven't even showed up yet.

He repeated the invitation. Golly, I said, I'm in pre-production, and I can't tear myself away, but thanks for the award. (No Dave, No Prize, he explained, and I stayed in Tahoe.)

The stupidest thing I've ever done in the film biz. (And I turned down *both* Scorsese's offer of *Raging Bull* and Sergio Leone's of *Once Upon a Time in America*.)

I was kvetching to my wife lately about this self-inflicted wound, and she said, "Nope, had you gone to Venice, we never would have met."

Advantage, Mamet.

The experience broke me of the habit of ascribing not only justice but legitimacy to any Awards.*

It's odd being accused—as regularly happened—of theft. The libels were sufficiently outlandish that my wonder, intermittently, dampened my outrage.

Two very successful producers sued me for fraud when I demanded they fulfill their contract; they alleged I'd cheated them, as I didn't apply scene numbers to my screenplay.†

---

*  I was nominated for two Oscars and won neither—a statistical impossibility.

†  No screenwriter puts in scene numbers—they are added in pre-production by the production department.

Harvey Weinstein contracted to pay me on a step-deal—for a first step of an outline. All the work in a screenplay is in the outline. If it's correct, the script, and most probably then the film, will work.

Further embellishment is just the Christmas ornaments—take 'em or leave 'em. In film they're dialogue (which film can do without), and the narrative material, of interest only to bored script readers, and home viewers who need to leave the room.

So Harvey asked to see my outline, and I said, fine, let's see the down payment.

"How would I know," he said, "that after I paid you, you wouldn't cheat me?"

"Alright," I said, "*you* write the fucking outline."


*Two Masterpieces.*

The Burghers of Amsterdam commissioned Rembrandt to commemorate a Company of Civic Guardsmen. *The Night Watch* (1642) is one of the world's greatest paintings. The buyers said that Rembrandt cheated them.

The honchos of another town reached out to commission Auguste Rodin. He sculpted *The Burghers of Calais*. They loathed it and held his payment in escrow.

The Société des Gens de Lettres, of Paris, hired him to honor Balzac. Rodin spent seven years on the statue until he understood the body to his satisfaction. He began with various nudes, and eventually draped the figure in a cloak.

The buyers saw the maquette and withheld his payment, as they said he was "dogging it." Kenneth Clark called it "the greatest piece of sculpture of the nineteenth century—perhaps, indeed, the greatest since Michelangelo."

Rodin spent seven years drawing studies of Balzac at various ages; he had clothing made to imitate Balzac's, and put his models in it. When the suits accused him of theft, he shattered the plaster maquette, revealing the musculature underneath.

# POODVECKER

My daughter Willa, who had a Czech nanny, first spoke English with a pronounced accent and many of the linguistic gaffes by which we're charmed in those foreigners we condescend to like.

Her favorite bird was the poodvecker.

Tolstoy, a Commie, points out that we know when a marriage is failing when the partners communicate in concise, straightforward sentences. Those spouses are in the process of reconstituting themselves as strangers. Divorce lawyers say it starts in bed and ends in court.

The eros and exuberance of filmmaking is extinguished 'neath the wet blanket of Good Works and Legalism, and the Family Language is forgot. What of the ancient "Whom do you have to fuck to get off of this movie?" And reference to film firearms as "gubs"—from Woody's bank robbery scene in *Take the Money and Run*. And so on. We see everywhere a terror of offending in those once functional relationships now all one breath away from "Get a lawyer."

After filming a scene, the sound guy once called for one minute of silence, to record room tone; and a crew member might suggest we sing the Sound Guy Hymn, "Him, Him, Fuck Him." But "fuck Him or Her" won't stretch. Farewell the poodvecker, Beloved Bird, farewell.

Directing actors is fairly simple. If it's a comedy, the answer is usually "Throw it away quicker"; for a drama, "Knock it off."

Acting schools load the actor with analyses that clarify nothing. They serve only to kill spontaneity, as the actor tries to remember which particular emotion or memory he is supposed to
associate with which word. Actors understand the scenes when
they first read them (just like you and me)—further analysis is
pointless. The scene is either: a recognition, leave-taking, confron-
tation, ultimatum, apology, proposal, appeal, reconciliation—and
there are a few more, whose names will occur to the reader. That's
all, folks.

Billy Wilder's famous question, of a love scene: What keeps them
apart? The separation is the writer's job, that's built onto the scene.
The actor's job is to overcome the difficulties not of his *performance*
but OF THE SCENE.

Why would anyone (in "real life," if such there is) burden himself,
for instance, at a job interview, by remembering, "I must get this job
because my mother is dying of cancer"?

The actor's job, having taken the job, is to get on with it, *accept*
the difficulties (the scene), stand still, and say the stupid fricking
words. How Rare, O Daughters of Zion, are those who will act ac-
cordingly. Which is why we have directors.

The Greats—Billy Wilder, Preston Sturges, De Sica, Kobayashi,
Ozu, Mario Monicelli, Powell and Pressburger, Kubrick—directed
their casts as a great conductor leads the orchestra. The journeymen
and hacks, as the cartoon has it, just wave their baton till the music
stops, then turn around and bow.

How might one "learn" movie directing? Film schools accept
(that is, bilk) "directing" students. But one can no more learn film
directing from a class than one can learn knife fighting from a video.
The film school "student directors" are paying for the right to act in
a charade, holding their place through the ability to please those who
are, in effect, their employees.

How might one learn film directing? A more useful question,
"How do I make a movie?" And more useful still, "How do I make

*this* movie?"* How might one make a film without the possession of a sheepskin? How does one make a Romanian omelet? "First, steal two eggs." How does one make a film? First, get a camera.

Curiously, there is one in your pocket. Remove camera from pocket, make film. Doing so, one will learn *immediately* lessons that make no sense in a classroom. The light is too bright, too dim; the passersby are all looking at the camera; the traffic noise is drowning out the dialogue; the actor doesn't like my direction; I'm running out of daylight. Don't shoot the star's close-up at the end of the day, as he will be tired; keep your temper. And so on.

The lessons become ever clearer when one tries to cut the thing together. We find the eyeline is wrong, the light does not match, a shot has been fudged, there is no cutaway, THE SCENE DOESN'T WORK, I don't have an ending. And so on. Now you are actually learning. And you might recall the lessons when you set out to make the next film—because you've paid for them.

Actually, you will recall *some* of the lessons and learn to repeat, "Oh jeez, I've done it *again* . . ." All the while learning fascinating new things never to do again.

The boxing coach will teach you, "For chrissake, keep your *guard* up," but no matter how extended his instructions, the real lesson will come from your sparring partner.

I was having a drink with two retired cops, and every reminiscence ended with raucous laughter, and two observations, "Oh God, we had fun" and "The poor kids today will never know what they missed."

Well, that's age for you.

The Wright brothers first exhibited the airplane in France in 1908; Blériot flew the Channel in 1909, and I'm sure Wilbur and

---

* I'm sure there are classes in "Relationship Behavior." A more practical consideration is: What is the best way to live *with this person*? The question is unanswerable without thought of *the desire to do so*. This desire immediately places the attention on the *object* rather than the subject.

Orville shook their heads at the poor slob who had missed the Good Old Days.

The Wrights learned to fly by watching birds; early filmmakers by watching people, and our contemporaries by watching films. But study of films will only inform the aspiring director how to make *that* film. And he won't actually even learn that; for the shot, the cut, the effect he's watching may be the product of accident or compromise, or that mélange we might call genius.

Back at the ranch, in the 1946 *Razor's Edge*, Anne Baxter has fallen off the wagon in 1920s Paris; she's a degenerate lush. Now Ty Power, who knew her back in Lake Forest, has returned from Tibet, where he studied yoga. He gets her clean. Then he decides to marry her. Gene Tierney, who has long loved Ty, decides to break it up.

She invites Anne to her apartment, where she is having afternoon champagne. She offers some to Anne, who is now sober. Anne refuses. Gene has to leave the room and asks Anne to wait. Anne waits, and eventually looks over, across the room, at the bottle of champagne. We all wait, watching. How will it unfold?

Each time I watch the film, not only do I wait for her to take the drink, but I can't remember the sequence leading to it. So each time, I'm on the edge of my seat.

Master shot, Anne in the foreground, back to camera.

Champagne way over there, in a bucket near the window.

Pause pause pause.

Pause.

Then Anne starts to walk toward the bottle.

That's it.

It gets me every time.

Had the director, Edmund Goulding, gone about it in the Studio Way, we would have seen:

Master shot, Anne in the room.

Her POV, the bottle of champagne.

Close-up, Anne looking at the bottle.

XCU bottle.

XCU Anne.

Master shot, Anne starts to walk to the bottle.

Insert: the bottle, Anne's hand, picking it up. Etcetera.

But we can't know if the sequence as shot was a mistake. Perhaps Edmund Goulding shot the CU of Anne, and the insert of the bottle, and the shot was ruined.

It doesn't matter, for the sequence is genius and the credit goes to the director, whether he planned it or not, and whether or not he was there in the editing room. And if the film is a dud, he gets the blame. I love it.

The audience, watching the film for the first time, experiences a beautiful anticipation, paid off in an unforeseen but perfect conclusion. Seeing it for the second time, they not only recall the excitement of the anticipation but experience it again.

If the sequence were shot the brain-dead way, they would recall nothing—why would they? They'd experienced nothing. They saw a sequence of eight shots, and then she takes a drink. But they knew she was going to take a drink *all the time*. All they received from this sequence is unnecessary confirmation. So what?

To pay the audience off sequence by sequence is the wisdom of that great director Aristotle: if the end of the play must be both surprising and inevitable, how much more worthy to employ this knowledge *of the audience's consciousness* in each scene, and then in every contributory sequence. The master of this, of course, was Buster Keaton.

How does one study an audience's consciousness? The only way, on stage or screen, is to sit there with them while they watch your Baby dying.*

---

* An artistic failure, "in front of God and everybody," is devastating. There is, however, and unfortunately, no education in a hit. A craft practiced in a bureaucracy has, for its audience, superior bureaucrats. Graduates of film school learn little or nothing of practical use, but the diploma is valuable, as it certifies them as compliant.

I worked with Ricky Jay for forty years, and I got to direct his magic shows. But when there was actual magic discussed, I was dismissed from the conference. I begged him to teach me an effect. He finally gave in. He said that he would show me a simple card manipulation, and that when I could perform it better than it had ever been performed he would show me another. He also passed along the ancient vaudeville wisdom that you don't know your act until everything that could go

If we study films to learn how to make them, all our efforts must be imitative. What can we learn from great films? To think longer and be bold—not in "expressing ourselves" (whatever that means) but in delighting the audience. In order to do so, we have to understand how they think. Easy to begin, as we watch films ourselves. Though we can't effectively question our films' viewers, we may observe them, and we may question ourselves about others' films, asking not "How did they do that?" but "Why did I, the viewer, at such and such a point, sit up and take notice, drift away in thought, or open my mouth in surprise?"

Some folks are happy with a life making widgets or, indeed, packing them into boxes. Nothing wrong with that, I used to do it myself. One of the benefits of a repetitive job is that the mind is allowed to drift away and fantasize. These fantasies are, in effect, brilliant films; for don't we structure them with expectations and disappointments, examples of heroism and treachery, and happy endings either in the marriage bed or in front of the firing squad?

What might drive our knowledge or dramatic expertise clean out of our head? You should have been here in the *old* days.

In those old days, making *Spartan*, I got to lie on the floor of Val Kilmer's camper at wrap, at dawn, beyond fatigue, drinking Bloody Marys, half vodka, half V8, and half horseradish, while he explained the Commerce Clause. I got to spend a film full of nights in Jack Nicholson's trailer on *Postman*, listening to the most idiosyncratic of raconteurs.

I wrote a script for Costa-Gavras, which he hated. He sent me a very thick envelope, stuffed, as I could feel, with many handwritten

---

wrong with it has. But insulation from an actual, non-suborned audience can teach nothing. An invited dress rehearsal full of friends is useless as a gauge of the show—they're there to show support. A showing of a film for a bureaucratic committee can serve only to reveal those superiors' assessment of how the piece might affect their standing with their own superiors.

"Industry Artists" whose work is rejected by the Suits may feel outrage, but they are spared the more human—and useful—shame.

pages. I'd already received the message, as he hadn't called for a month after getting my beautiful script. So I didn't open the letter. I gave it to my agent, Howard Rosenstone, and called the next day.

"Did you read it?"

He said, "Yes."

"What did it say?"

"I'm not going to tell you."

# GIFTS

I'd learned, pre–show business, young and usually out of work, to assess new employers by their handshake on first meeting. As the Cake, so is the Wedding.

Later on, as such meetings were, supposedly, the conjunction of Equals, I elaborated on the insight.

I always brought a gift to a first meeting. It was, as in the Asian tradition, not of great monetary value (everyone can spend money if he has it) but a display of thoughtfulness on the part of the donor—that is, of that which actually *cost* the giver something: his time or his thought.

I was hired by Brian De Palma to write *The Untouchables*.

I'm a Chicago South Sider. My grandparents' generation lived in Capone's South Side, and some of them knew him and told me about him. I wrote a treatment for De Palma prior to meeting him, and went shopping.

I found a contemporary bio of Capone, in a rare edition, signed by the author. I had it wrapped and went to our first meeting.

"Hi, hi," and "sit down," he said. As I sat, I handed him the package. "I brought you something," I said. He put it aside, saying, "I have a problem with your Scene Two."

And so it went. Up to and including Bob De Niro calling me from Canada to kvetch about a scene. "You read it before you took the part," I said. "Yes," he said. "Why'd it get worse just because you have to act it?" I said. And that was it, for ten silent years (during which he did four of the films I wrote, God bless him).*

---

* After our reconciliation, I wrote a script intended for him, *The Edge*. (The part was, in the event, played beautifully by Alec Baldwin.) I sent the script to Bob. He

153

After *The Untouchables* I'd bought a BMW (a German car), and I loved it till I sat at a stoplight and in the adjacent lane was Brian De Palma, in the same car. That was the end of my relationship with BMW.

I was asked to do a five-hour MasterClass on writing, directing,

---

requested a table read. (NB: No script was ever made by anyone requesting a table read, but I granted graciously what I dared not refuse.)

After the read, Bob came to me and said, "I like it, but I don't love it. It's very good, but it's just not a thing I have to do, and I've only got so many of them left in me. Are you mad at me?"

Me: "No, of course not."

Bob: "You're sure?"

Me: "Yes."

Bob: "Good, cause, I want to ask a favor. I've got this piece of shit I'm supposed to start shooting on Monday. Could you take a look at the script?"

and general theatrical aesthetics. I went kicking and screaming and had the time of my life. It was produced by Erica Kammann and Matthew Rutler and directed by Diane Houslin. They and their team turned what I thought would be three days of drudgery into a joy. They'd gone to my archives at UT Austin and had re-created (forged) actual notebooks of mine; they'd gone to my cabin in Vermont and had re-created it as a set. (NB: the forging is one of the excellences of the Archives folk in Texas; they guard the originals and make duplicates that would deceive the woman at the DMV.)

At the end of the show, I began talking about *The Demolished Man*. This is a 1953 science fiction book by Alfred Bester. In it, telepaths advertise testing for those who believe they have the power. The applicants line up, waiting for their turn to be examined, but, unseen, the actual telepaths are watching them from above and thinking: "*If you can hear me, please go through the door on the left marked EMPLOYEES ONLY.*" Once in a long while an applicant shakes his head and hesitantly walks through the prohibited door.

Well, it was at the end of a three-day shoot, I was exhausted and I had the flu—both offered in extenuation of my behavior; for when I finished my story (and thus the shoot), I started to cry. I asked for another take, apologized to the crew, and in this take cried a little less, and they used it.

I believe the last time I cried was at *Random Harvest*, starring Ronald Colman and Greer Garson. (Filmed 1942, tears 1970.)

We finished the MasterClass shoot, and a week later there arrived a signed first edition of *The Demolished Man*.

# HOW MAX FACTOR BECAME PREGNANT

The first silent filmmakers dealt awkwardly with lighting. Subjects of still photographs wore no makeup, and one had no difficulty making out their features. But actors onstage slathered their faces. A still photo can be held near the face, but the back row of the theater needs to make out the actor's eyes and lips.

Theatrical makeup survived in early film, as the actors and directors all came from the stage. The makeup's not so jarring on the actresses—women have always made up for effect, onstage and off-. But many actors wear heavy lipstick in silents and in early talkies. These are black-and-white films, and it's reasonable to assume early directors wanted to make the actors' lips look more red.

However, red in black-and-white goes black. It took a while for the black-lipped actors to come to the directors' attention, from which we might assume that the director's job ended when he yelled "cut," and that he didn't see the assembled film till its triumphant sneak in Fresno.

Makeup was also used on the stars to correct, enhance, or in fact obliterate features thought in need of alteration. Merle Oberon, an Anglo-Indian, had her hairline raised and her skin lightened to make her look more European. African American actors had their skin darkened to make them unmistakably less so. Joan Crawford's eyebrows were shaved and replaced with huge painted crescents.

Many stars had their noses straightened by the ancient stage technique of highlights and shadows.

Today, as of old, an on-screen lovely will awake, fresh and stretching, in the Early Morn, and we are all the better able to appreciate her beauty, as she's wearing ten pounds of eye makeup, and eyelashes longer than Peter O'Toole's in *Lawrence of Arabia*. (The reference intended for the film but also applicable to its Hero, who enjoyed dressing up.)\*

Al Pacino plays Phil in *Phil Spector*. In his mansion hangs a portrait of Lawrence. Al shows the house to his lawyer, Helen Mirren, and explains that Lawrence was 5'2", liked little boys, probably wasn't even in the army, and won World War I. J. Edgar Hoover, we are told, liked wearing a tutu, but everybody enjoys a change. That's why we went to the movies.

Wise exploitation of the close-up changed the relationship between Lighting and Makeup. Cinematic inventors shaped the face through lights and shadows, and the camera's proximity required the invention of new, non-oil or wax-based, makeup.

Maksymilian Faktorowicz came to America from Poland in 1904. He was born near Lodz, just like my grandparents. This, in the Jewish world, is called *yicchus*, or "descent," which can be claimed not only genealogically but through any connection, however remote or, indeed, fanciful.

We always held that Audrey Hepburn was Jewish because we wanted her to be. She was not, but Katharine (noted elsewhere) was, her original family name Hebron. And she had bad skin. No problem onstage, where there were no close-ups, but her film work needed Max Factor. He not only created makeup for her, Jean Harlow, and all the greats of the Golden Age, he created Makeup. He coined the term to sell the mascara and eye pencils he produced for the movies, and was the first to market it to the general public. Much of the *ruse de guerre* of the war between the sexes (now carried out as Diplomacy by Other Means) was created by Max for the films.

Much modern technology comes to us from the military—or, as our more squeamish time would have it, the Space Program. The Flickers were the Space Program of sexuality and courting. As

---

\*  At the premiere, Noël Coward told O'Toole that had he been any prettier the film should be retitled *Florence of Arabia*.

Tolstoy told us, the kids exchange the salacious and taboo at school, bring it home, and corrupt the parents. (Some think that it was, in fact, their children who taught the pirates to go "Arrrghhh . . .")

Max came from my people's neck of the woods, as did Helena Rubinstein. Chaja Rubinstein was born near Kraków. She and her family moved to Australia in the 1890s. She carried some jars of face cream in her luggage, the Natives down under were entranced and wanted some. She began making face cream with the lanolin that, we may assume, was otherwise a glut on the market there, and one thing led to another. She made a huge fortune and gave much of it away.

My particular connection is through Maximilian furs.

They're still around today, a worldwide brand name. But when I was associated, they were a family-owned outfit—the most prestigious of furriers in the poshest of showrooms in Manhattan, their clients the superrich, royalty, and movie stars.

Mme Potok was the owner and designer. She was the mother of my friend Andy. When I was other than affluent, in New York, I would occasionally drop by her showroom, fortuitously, at lunchtime, and find her in her office with a tuna sandwich, and she'd have her people make me one, too. She and her family were the grandest furriers in Warsaw. They left one day ahead of the Nazis and were eventually admitted to the United States through the auspices of Helena Rubinstein.

It was Mme Potok who told me that she'd asked her benefactor, "Helena, what is it you really sell? You aren't actually selling anything of use, it's just inert white cream," and Mme Rubinstein said, "I'm selling the most precious thing in the world. I'm selling hope."


It's the oddest thing, being married.

I look at my wife and see a smiling, graceful beauty. Over the years, I've come to think, "Ah, that's what *we* look like." But it's not what *I* look like. My reflection in the mirror is familiar, but that's not

what I look like, either—that image is backward. When it's flipped
to accuracy, through an iPad or photograph, I seem to myself misshapen.

The movies also offer beauty through distortion. Attempts in film
to make people look "more real" seem, some small time later, as foolish as painting the silent star's lips red. The movies are an abstraction
from our consciousness, which itself is an abstraction of what may
or may not be an ultimate reality. Stanislavski imported palm trees
to dress a tropic set in Moscow, and onstage they of course looked
fake. Because they were real. /

Theatrical Realism, at the turn of the century, was the depiction
of unpleasant or unfortunate *actions* and situations: poverty, alcoholism, adultery. On-screen—as developments in the camera out-
shone the stodgy old script—it came to mean the offer of shocking
*images*: fake blood, real or faked sex, pyrotechnics, car crashes, the
cartoon destruction of whole worlds, and so on. But these are no
more "real" than *Gidget Goes Hawaiian*. They just employ a different mode of artifice.

I began writing plays at the end of the Kitchen Sink period. In the
fifties, the presence of the sink, or the paterfamilias in an undershirt,
gave the imprimatur to drama and films that Diversity does today—
they were a fashionable gimmick touted (or even understood) as a
closer approach to Reality.

In 1997's *Good Will Hunting*, Matt Damon, a mathematics prod-
igy from Southie, is urged by his best friend, Ben Affleck, to escape
the Old Neighborhood, with its (unspecified) aridities, take his talent, and flee. From what?

This last hurrah of the Kitchen Sink called on the audience to
accept that the Neighborhood Life was somehow bad—and that the
Hero's gift could only be enjoyed in Berkeley or some other intel-
lectual Paradise. The Kitchen Sink reappears now as the "life in the
hood" films of the Black or Hispanic Experience. In another generation the children of these filmmakers, now affluent, will regard this
as a foreign experience.

Leon Uris wrote *Exodus*, a cri de coeur of Judaism; his grandchildren are probably writing for *South Park*.

All film is an alteration, not only employing light and sound in the service of fantasy but playing upon our consciousness, such that we accept the manipulated as "true to life." But all film is manipulated by its creators—actors, directors, designers, and editors.*

If the film is actually a product of The Script (Ricky played the villain Gupta in the James Bond film *Tomorrow Never Dies* and reported that there *was* no script, that the actors were called day by day to improvise a scene), the uber-manipulation is the director's vision. If it is a good script, the film is his vision not of Life but of the *Script*.

The self-deluded feel they "have a script in them," not realizing that it's in them, as they have neglected to write it down. Should they actually do so, they will hate it, as it will have nothing to do with how it felt when it was "in them." They may then attempt to wrestle the thing closer to The Feeling they had, but they'll never get it closer, as the feeling, which *felt* like an idea, was only a feeling—their attempts are like a chef saying he wanted to make the couscous taste like the First Day of School.

The good script is the triumph of wretched persistence over narcissism. In its enjoyment, the audience is freed of the curse of their consciousness by the *author*, who lugged that burden up the hill.

Many movie stars seem misshapen when viewed up close. My friend Daniel said that Bette Davis had the largest head he'd ever seen. One can discern a certain attractive prognathism in, for example, Burt Lancaster, and I will not mention Clark Gable's ears. But the camera, like our mirror reflection, might *like* some of these deformities, and so do we viewers. Just as we enjoy the reassembled deformities of the writer's mind.

The year 1964 was graced by two masterpieces, *Fail Safe* and

---

* Documentaries are no more "real" than features—they're just movies.

*Dr. Strangelove*—Sid Lumet, and Stanley Kubrick, respectively. The stories are identical. A nuclear strike is inadvertently launched against Russia, and the President and All His Men must avert disaster.

*Fail Safe* is horrifying, and *Dr. Strangelove* the funniest film ever made. They are renditions of the same imaginary but possible event, and both are true. What, then, is Realism? Well, one might say, don't be disingenuous; it is, of course, the attempt to get close to an observed reality. But what testimony is more impeachable than that of an Eyewitness?*

Art forms distort what we call perception into a new reality. Nothing is truer than Beethoven's Fifth Symphony, but what does it "mean"?

Max and Helena were household names in the twentieth century. Their brands endure, their names are no longer part of our current speech. But they were.

Schoolyard joke, circa 1955.

A. Did you hear Helena Rubinstein got pregnant?

B. Yeah?

A. Max Factor.

A cultural artifact, of interest only to the Urban Archaeologist. And to genius.

I shared the joke, as I do all those of my youth, with my son, Noah.

"Yeah, that's funny, Dad," he said—a complete dismissal—"but I can make it better."

"Go on," I said.

"Did you hear Max Factor got pregnant?"

"Yeah?"

"Helena Rubinstein."

---

* See the irreconcilable differences in political opinion, each side convinced not that its opponents are wrong but that they are insane.

# THINGS CHANGE

George Beau Brummell (1778–1840) was the most famous of the Regency Fops. He was great friends with the Prince of Wales, the future George IV. His name today is a byword for The Dandy, which he was, but he was petted, in his day, because of his wit. He came late to some rendezvous and explained that he'd hurt his leg. "And," he said, "it was my favorite leg."

During the Vietnam War, an anonymous soldier was immemorialized by a phrase still part of Military vocabulary. The soldier was on the radio to Command when he came under fire and exclaimed, "What the *fuck* . . ."

His commander scolded him, "Say again, using proper radio procedure, over." The soldier responded, "What the fuck, over."

An agent, now deceased, well known to us all, hired a young secretary. At the end of her first day, he offered to drive her home. They took winding Mulholland Drive; and he began to drive aggressively; she asked him to slow down, and he sped up; she pleaded she was becoming frightened, and he said, "Show me your tits or I'll kill us both."

Memorable phrases from my own film career follow.

I first met Paul Newman at Sidney's office, during pre-production for *The Verdict*. I said, "Hello." He replied, "I just got laid."

Ben Gazzara played the Bad Guy Associate of Becca Pidgeon's villain in our *Spanish Prisoner*.

At our first meeting, I said, "Glad to meet you," and he said, "I've never been able to penetrate an Italian woman."

Down the list, but a small footnote to history, is our pre-Oscar party for *The Verdict*. We were invited to David Brown's house in Malibu: myself, James Mason, Sidney, and Paul.

David was married to Helen Gurley Brown (*Sex and the Single Girl*, 1964). Walking up to the house, Sidney said, "She'll insult you within twenty seconds." She greeted us, said hello to Sidney, James, and Paul, and asked me, "What do *you* do . . . ?"

And I believe it was Samuel Goldwyn Jr. (producer of my film *Oleanna*) who said, of my script, "The enormous respect I have for your talent does not permit me to do anything but puke over this piece of shit." He hated both the script and the film, but he was a charming man, and spoke lovingly of George Cukor, who, he said, was his cherished surrogate father. God bless them both.

The Communist International was the Bolshevik Apparat promoting world Marxism. It was known at the Comintern; and Cukor's group as the Homintern. A philologist might treasure the bon mot as evidence of the universality of Communist thought in Hollywood. This interest was just fashion. The randy, drunk, doped, crazed-by-greed, and be-fantasized movie folk took to Communism then as today they "fight global warming."

McCarthy landed on Hollywood Reds, hounding various for their publicity value, and probably drove more folk to suicide than drugs *or* the films of Ingmar Bergman.

There weren't a lot of yoks coming out of the blacklist, but Lucille Ball was called to testify before McCarthy's Senate Committee, and Desi defended her with "The only thing red about Lucy is her hair, and *that's* fake."

The Hollywood humor of my day was sex humor.

What does a teamster girl say after sex: "Where are you guys from?" How do you know a teamster has died: "His wife picks up his checks."

And always indictable were producers and, of course, agents.

This, told of Mike Ovitz:

Young woman gets into an elevator with Ovitz.

She asks, "How about a blow job?" He responds, "What's in it for me . . . ?"

The joke certainly goes back to the dawn of the movies, and probably dates back to ancient Rome.

I got off a few good things in my time.* And put them in the movies. I did it for a living.

We remember our youth as pleasure or noble struggle and dramatize the infirmities of age as injustice.

The movie biz of my time was an adventure—the culture was raunchy, ribald, and energizing; it held the promise of any next moment bringing love, sex, money, fame, artistic challenge, or an encounter with the highwaymen.

But of course things do change. The culture of Hollywood today resembles that of my youth as little as a PTA meeting calls to mind a fire in a whorehouse. Simultaneous with a raid. The workers and the thugs, in my time, were many things, but I do not recall that we were sententious.

---

* Bruce Berman was head of something or other at Warners some time back. I'd been working with Randy Newman, my hero, on a libretto of his *Faust*. Bruce wanted Randy and me and Lorne Michaels to come by Warners and pitch something or other. It may have been *Faust*, I don't remember. In any case, in we went.

Bruce was forty-five minutes late for the meeting, and showed up with still-wet mustard on his tie. "Well," he said, "it's such a pleasure to meet you three, especially you, Randy, as I 'was' you for a while. When the Beatles first came to New York, I figured they'd very likely known your music, but didn't know *you*; so I went to their hotel, told them I was you, and palled around with them for a week. Now . . .

"It's absurd that *I* would ask you, Randy, you, Lorne, and you, Dave, to 'audition' a project for me, but what the hell, not everyone likes Mexican food . . ."

He turned to me, as it was the "Writer's Turn."

Pause pause.

"What the fuck do you mean," I said, "'not everyone likes Mexican food'?"

That closed the meeting. Out in the hall Randy suggested I'd just cost him a quarter of a million bucks. And I was sincerely contrite. But *hey* . . .

MU**III**ON
FOR
PUNISHMENT

"MUTTON II - RAISES THE BAA
ON THE SHEEP-ACTION GENRE"
NY TYNZE

# AN APPRECIATION
# OF THE STATE OF PLAY

The artist's problem, as always, is that the merchants, indispensable to our sustenance, and the parasites who batten on us have no idea what we are doing. Those self-pressed into service of The Industry are like the inspired automotive designers, fresh out of school, snapped up by Detroit automakers to sketch fuel door covers.

The American auto industry was changed by the Japanese and Germans, starting in 1945 from zero (thanks to Douglas Aircraft and Boeing), and by the hot-rodders in SoCal who remodeled Detroit's guff into something cool.

Our obliteration of their manufactories gave our postwar new friends, the Germans and the Japanese, that which GM could never have: a clean sheet of paper. And the Pacific Coast car freaks had the artist's only other requirement: inspiration bordering on mania, NEXT TO WHICH NOTHING AT ALL MATTERED. The hot-rodders wouldn't have traded the life of sun, sex, and auto mechanics for the highest-paid position in Detroit; they would have pitied the stock-optioned Executives, had they ever thought of them.

Artists who don't hold "producers" in contempt—absent the remote possibility of their having demonstrated a simple decent regard for a contract—are nuts. One must protect oneself from the effects of unashamed greed for money *or* acceptance. We all would appreciate help in taking our pigs to market, but a human desire for acceptance—in effect, a self-delusion—often blinds us to those pigs' identity.

Orson Welles was immensely fortunate in having, as his producer, my friend John Houseman. He also had Franchot Tone, a very wealthy actor, who funded much of the Mercury Theatre.

I wrote a film for John Frankenheimer, who confessed himself not only pleased but grateful, and suggested we do many more together. But he died.

Here's a story from the world of Aviation.

A friend of mine is an old Freight Dog pilot with more than twenty thousand hours. He flew in the military. He also flew charters, for a while, for the Great of Hollywood. There he was, schlepping a very famous Producer known for his War Films. As they were approaching their destination, the Producer wandered up to the cockpit and said to my friend, "Don't you think you should put the flaps down?" My friend said, "Sir, I am flying the plane, and I need you to go back and sit down."

They were getting off the plane, and the Producer said to my friend, "I don't think I like your attitude." My friend said, "Sir, have you ever flown a plane?" The Producer said, "No, but I have many hours in a simulator."

My friend said, "Sitting in a simulator has as little relation to flying a plane as making a war movie has to actual combat."

The Producer said, "I don't know they're that dissimilar."

"Fuck you, you draft-dodging swine," my friend replied.

If we look up Bob Evans on the internet we find umpteen entries for a sausage manufacturer. *My* Bob Evans, when head of production at Paramount, was, curiously, not turning out sausages but making some stunning movies, e.g., *The Godfather, Rosemary's Baby, Serpico, True Grit,* and *Chinatown.* His autobiography, *The Kid Stays in the Picture,* is a hoot.

In it we find, among other self-serving lies (what else would one expect in an autobiography), his admission that he snuck down to a screening room every evening and corrected Coppola's errors in *The Godfather*. And wasn't I myself addressed by some unknown gent, at the next urinal, after the first screening of *The Verdict*?

He: "Like the film?"

Me: "Yes."

He: "I wrote it."

*Can* anyone be as gormless as these producers? How might one understand them? Better to understand oneself: the Pig who can find a truffle; and the companion on his journey, the producer, irritated by his constant digging in the earth, who turns him into roast pork.

We read in Proverbs that he who increases wisdom increases sorrow. The equation is commutative; that is, it can be read in either direction with equal profit.

We not only become sad because we have gained wisdom; we gain wisdom because, and only because, we have been saddened.

The wisdom, then, is on offer, and we are free to accept it or not. Acceptance is anguishing, as it entails a rethinking of the nature of the world, and of our place in it.

The tragedy of loss, betrayal, and recognition of our shame, hurt, and folly challenges us to face this otherwise avoidable truth: that the test does not begin until we are assured that the test is over and we have failed. This is the mechanism of all dramatic tragedy. If the Hero is not bludgeoned into acceptance of defeat, there can be no third act.

The above will now be familiar to any who have hit bottom, and familiar later to all but the very few (fortunate or not, you say) exempted.

Of course, the most exhilarating thing is to lead men into combat, to command a ship, and, in the civilian world, to direct a film. It's an incomparable privilege that I've enjoyed for forty years.

The joy consisted in the *unrestricted* opportunity to explore the relationship between cause and effect.

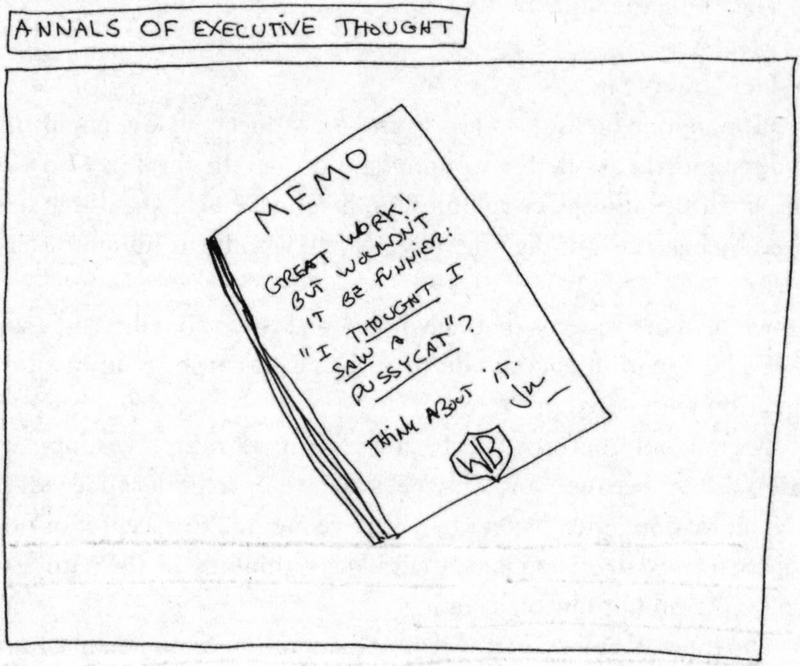
ANNALS OF EXECUTIVE THOUGHT
MEMO
GREAT WORK! BUT WOULDN'T IT BE FUNNIER: "I THOUGHT I SAW A PUSSYCAT"?
THINK ABOUT IT.
WB

# THE CARDS

I was a young fellow in Chicago in the early seventies. Our theater company was the St. Nicholas. We supported it through outside straight jobs. Macy and I were waiters at a gay restaurant, Patricia Cox was a B-girl at a local bar, and I don't recall what Steve Schachter did but it will occur to me as we go to press.

The neighborhood (Halsted and Addison) loved and supported us, and we were opposed by the *Chicago Tribune*, in the person of its drama critic, Roger Dettmer. There was an alternative newspaper, the *Reader*, whose critics came to our defense. These included Michael Feingold, who later went to the *Voice* (and was influential in getting me the Pulitzer Prize for *Glengarry* in 1984), a friend in the true Chicago tradition, and Michael VerMeulen.

VerMeulen had dropped out of school at fourteen and walked into the *Reader* offices, handed them a phony résumé, and demanded a job. *Obiter dictum*: ALL theatrical and film résumés MUST contain attractive lies. These are the equivalent of the Big Hair of TV evangelists: one has to stop the eye of the buyer. No kidding. Tell them you were a Forest Ranger in Alberta. Who's going to check?

In any case, VerMeulen was our friend and champion. He later took over as editor of British *GQ*. He died young. He was the real thing. In any case, he championed us in the true Chicago tradition, which is, "Fuck it, you're right. And if you're not right, fuck it anyway."

In some interview I referred to Roger Dettmer as "an asshole,"* and the comment found its way into print. Dettmer responded, in the *Tribune*, saying that I'd used a word unsanctioned in polite discourse. I wrote him my apology: that of course he was not an asshole. He was *like* an asshole.

These were the days before computers. Newspaper copy was hacked out at typewriters and carried by copyboys to the compositor's room. I schemed with Schachter to have one of us from the St. Nicholas hired as copyboy; when given a "Kill this play" review by Dettmer, we would swap it out for one of our own composition and rush that to the presses. But we never got around to it. And computers took the place of typewriters.

Aha, but as the fingernail heals, the quick beneath recalls the

---

* For the artist all criticism is devastating, and no praise is sufficient. One might remind oneself that criticism comes from paid detractors, these, of necessity, talentless and otherwise unemployable. But our umbrage at criticism of our dog is not lessened by the critic's profession as a breeder.

A blind pig, we know, can find a truffle. And a critic whose only excellence is an unabashed readiness to indict his betters can come to a conclusion about our work's shortcomings that we may in fact share. Which only makes the affront worse.

Here it is as if our private practices are being broadcast to the world not only by a Peeping Tom but by one *who is only guessing*, although he may be guessing correctly. Samuel Johnson said the censure of knaves and fools is applause: a phrase rendered in the vernacular as "Fuck 'em all but six for pallbearers, and fuck them, too."

What other attitude might one adopt? For if we accept as helpful the loathsome (if accurate) gossip of fools, have we not joined their number?

Yes and no. The truth hurts, and by that pain we may identify its accuracy.

Impertinence may offend but it cannot humiliate. A better man than I would kiss the rod. But I am not a better man, and so my strategy is to read no criticism. This, though profoundly moral, is a pointless choice, as the power of indictment is the power of salaciousness, which, like murder, will out.

E.g., "Dave, it's appalling what X wrote about your last film. How *dare* they say _____." And, as always, "Here we are, in Boise, all moved in. We enclose this from the local paper, which you may have missed."

And there is always that superglacial silence on the morning after the failed opening.

Two notable fan offerings: "I'm a great fan of yours. Great, great, very very great." And the horror of the Other Name: "You're one of my favorite filmmakers: you and _____," the last a perpetrator of works with which no rational being would wipe his ass.

wound; just so, the mind, affronted by (you-know-whoms), may callous, while the affront remains, awaiting reactivation.

This, in my case, came with the Cards.

Back then, in the '70s, film audiences went to sneaks at Bakersfield or somewhere and were invited, upon their exit, to fill out cards, cataloguing their opinion of what they had seen. These responses were most heavily relied upon by Studio Executives, insufficiently hip to consider that they were less views of The Movie than records of those flattered into casting themselves as Film Critics. Many such jotted down, as did the professionals, their proclamations as to "what a person like oneself, now a critic, might think of a film like the one just viewed, in reasonable hope of endorsement from the notionally like-minded."

Why, hell, I thought, it's just like Roger Dettmer.

I never learned to play chess past "how do the pieces move," but did read that advanced players did not think "five moves ahead" but, rather, recognized the similarities between the board's position at the moment and the games they had played and studied.

With the Cards, here I was, looking, once again, at Roger Dettmer.

When one had turned out a magnificent low-budget film, the budget guaranteed that the distributing entity would, having good hope of recouping its initial investment, be unlikely to shell out more than chump change on promotion. Unless the CARDS were so overwhelming as to portend . . . etcetera. But I never got around to that scam, either.*

---

* Here is all you need to know about Hollywood. There is not and never has been any correlation between audience testing and box office.

Joe Farrell was the king of audience testing from the late seventies till his death in 2011. He used audience cards, surveys, and electronic testing, among other means.

In the last, the chosen participants would sit in a booth and screen the film. They'd each have two knobs, one for each hand. One was turned to indicate "excitement" or some such, and the other to indicate "enjoyment of the scene." The responses were displayed on graphs to the filmmakers, indicating the age and sex of the testees.

Joe did the research on several of my films. I asked him, after one screening, how the cards looked. He said, "Mixed"; I said I wished the numbers were higher, and he said, "How high would you like them to be?"

A smarter man than I would have shelled out.

Nor to the oft suggested writing of two screenplays. One for the making of the film, and another for the diversion of the script readers.

To actually make the film:

FADE IN:

DAWN. OPEN SEA. SEABIRDS LANDING ON A MASS OF DRIFTWOOD. CAMERA MOVES IN TO REVEAL IT IS A MAKESHIFT RAFT, TO WHICH IS HANGING MORTON GRAVES, A FORTY-YEAR-OLD NEAR-NAKED MAN.

And the script reader's studio version:

LITTLE DID MORTON GRAVES THINK, WHEN SETTING OUT TO DISCOVER THE LOST ATOLL OF BORAGAVORA, THAT THE ERRATIC COURSE OF AN INTER-ISLAND STEAMER, CAPTAINED BY A DRUNKEN LOUT, WOULD SLICE THE BOW OFF HIS LUXURY YACHT.

That's right.

I should have done it. And, as a prolific author, I should have adopted, forty years ago, several pen names, under each of which I could appeal, not to a different audience, but to the benign neglect of various unangered critics. For the question of those enraged by productivity was, "Who did I think I was . . . ?" Whose very vehemence was an indictment of their talentless, loveless, drab, and pointless lives.

I attended one Oscars and one Emmys, nominated, each time (*The Verdict*, *Phil Spector*), but came away sadly disappointed in the judges' ruling.

But I should not have been, for theirs was the same as those committees who ruled MOST LIKELY TO SUCCEED. Their choice fell upon one most likely not to succeed but most obviously to *have* succeeded in those endeavors thought praiseworthy in a dedicated high school student.

Give me the ne'er-do-wells, every time. I've never met a stupid audience, but bureaucrats and their mob-think make me sick.

# A TWO-SIDED COIN

The neighborhood theaters and comedy venues of my youth sold iconoclasm, and so attracted those of that bent; that would be me. How grateful was I? How grateful was the closeted mid-century lone homosexual of Birch Falls, Idaho, who discovered Fire Island? That lucky fellow wasn't ever going "home." Me neither.

The Theater, and my first decades in Film, had no downside. I'd found a meritocracy that appreciated what I had not ever realized were skills. Who wouldn't work, work being more fun than fun?*

Work and talent (and luck) are a good recipe for success, which breeds isolation, and for prosperity, which both encourages luxury and requires either financial sagacity (a rare extra talent in the artist) or the aid of Advisors and Managers, these professions attractive (inter alia) to toadies, parasites, and thieves. The stories abound.

Not only does this turn into that over time, it is the *definition* of time.

The "support positions" listed above could also be described, by the dyspeptic, as parasitical. But all life is parasitical, in that it lives off other life. "Scout" can mean either to investigate or to avoid, and growth means progression toward death.

But on my side of the fence I must shake my head at the support positions sheltering those who, though they have a right to live, could perhaps employ that right other than in fucking up my films.

---

* Noël Coward.

Some contemporary wildlife biologists hold that it's the hyenas who pull down the prey, and the Lazy Lions who chase them off to snack on it. The horror of parasites is that their successes lead to increased breeding, which must lead to a depletion of the host mechanisms, and *then* what do the poor parasites do? Starved and confused, they will be prey to some new Masters called into being by the abundant free lunch. (See films advertising twenty producers.)

A grand artifact of the nineties is the good news/bad news jokes. Good news: your teeth are fine; bad news: your gums will have to come out. The joke seems to be a recognition of a philosophic truth. The Jews understand that the Good News *is* the Bad News. For Good News (prosperity, success, or safety) *will* attract the notice of the Cossacks. The nonreligious understanding is, curiously, more metaphysical. Jews do not fear the notice of God in success—we understand God as one who desperately wants us to do well. We just fear humans.

Sailors, actors, and filmmakers—we insulate ourselves against a Greater Power by superstitious practice. We fear, not God, but the previous holders of the position: the gods. I will not venture near the edge by naming them here—the Greeks called them the Honored Ones; they are those who are summoned not by the enjoyment but by the *announcement* of Good Fortune.

There I was in London, directing my play *Bitter Wheat*, starring John Malkovich as the Weinstein-Inspired Mogul. We'd just missed each other in Chicago. His Steppenwolf Theatre took over the space of our St. Nicholas when Macy and I went to New York. We'd never worked together, and I don't think we'd ever met. But he signed on to play the part in the West End, and I was happy as a clam.

There we were, in his dressing room, in previews, discussing various aspects of the production and our hopes for the run. I noted that, frequently, I was knocking on wood, and that he was, at the same points, doing the same. I was told by an Old Jew that it is a plea, through the True Cross, for the intercession of Jesus. I continued it anyway, as I can use all the help I can get.

I flew to Miami Beach in 2002 to talk to Denzel Washington. He'd read my script for *Spartan*, a paramilitary thriller, and asked me to come by and talk. At the end of the evening, he said that, yes, he'd be glad to play the lead. But that he might have an idea or two, and would I be open to hearing them. "Of course," I said. "I need all the help I can get." This last was delivered rather slurred because of too much liquid cheer. And off I staggered.

The next day Denzel's agent informed me that he had changed his mind. I understood. We were Two Guys talking, about a Job, and then I'd cracked out of turn. It was not that I'd said I needed all the help I could get; it was that it wasn't true. I was then no longer a filmmaker but a dread sycophant, to whom he, rightly, shouldn't trust his time.

The good news is that I went on to make *Spartan* with Val Kilmer, who was magnificent, and a treat; and Denzel, in its stead, made *Man on Fire*, a smashing film by Tony Scott, whose ending I fixed, while watching it on DVD.*

---

\* In the film's final sequence, Denzel, a bodyguard, goes to ransom the child kidnapped under his care. He is shot at the beginning of the sequence but continues onto the bridge to complete the transfer. He negotiates to trade himself—that is, his life—for the return of the girl. She runs to her mom, Radha Mitchell, and Denzel is driven off to his death by the kidnappers. *But* as he was already dying at the beginning of the transfer, his self-sacrifice is moot.

They missed a beat, as Denzel might have agreed to trade his life for that of the kid while *planning* to escape. We might wonder at his easy acquiescence, and then realize that he is about to FOOL them. Aha, and well in line with his resourcefulness. THEN, his plan goes bad—he gets shot and must actually give up his life in order to save the little girl. But everyone's a critic.

We all make mistakes. Billy Wilder said that every director leaves the set thinking, on his way home, "*Now* I know how to direct that scene today." Warners made the funniest cartoons of all time. Chief among them was the Road Runner. The only dialogue involved was the hero's "Beep Beep." Late in the run someone decided that Wile E. Coyote should talk. The cartoon was ruined, as we are saddened by his newfound ability.

# THE CENTIPEEP

The great Ira Levin wrote a real silly book called *The Boys from Brazil*. The gag was that escaped Nazis, fled to Brazil, planned to bring back the Third Reich.

Here's how: they were going to breed a bunch of new Hitlers. These would be fashioned from mothers and fathers having some of the same characteristics of our Adolf's folks. The kids would grow in environments similar to those that formed him and would undergo signal Life Events just like those of Der Führer's childhood.

We hear that Barbra Streisand has cloned her favorite dog so she can have a close approximation of it around again after the original's allotted span. My genetic notion is this: folks like leg of lamb. A sheep only has four legs; crossbreeding with a centipede would give us the CENTIPEEP.

These examples take no account of Environmental Variables. One cannot supply all the influences formative of Young Adolf— Mr. Levin's hobbyists could only pick a few. And Ms. Streisand's dog's beloved personality was formed by its constant interaction, for good or ill, with her *at a previous age*. However much she loved Woofy II, or, God willing, III, a ninety-year-old owner isn't going to play the same amount of fetch as a forty-year-old.

We have two poodles. My wife said she wanted the sort of dog that, "if you walk it, it dies." But we got our two standards, who are, I am sure, as demanding as various unnamed Stars. And why not? They are retrievers. They were bred to hunt. If we go swimming with them, they treat us as they would a duck—that is, they want to bite us and carry us to shore. That's what they're bred for, and it's tough to beat genetics.

Is Bad Behavior an inevitable concomitant of talent? The old stage adage has it: "In a Star it's temperament, in a chorus girl it's bad manners."

I worked with several actors, though dissuaded beforehand by colleagues who'd experienced them.

I was told Val Kilmer was impossible. He was a pussycat.

Respected director friends cautioned me against Alec Baldwin. Filming with him was a delight. (He starred with Anthony Hopkins in *The Edge*, and I directed him in my *State and Main*.)

I did encounter several folks, before and behind the camera, who had an other than grand attitude, but I was warned against *none* of them.

What can it mean? Perhaps it has something to do with temperament, and it certainly has something to do with mutual confidence. Which of us wants to put himself in the hands of someone who doesn't know what he's doing, who is unprepared, untrustworthy, duplicitous, or false?

An actor, in this situation, is like one on a disastrous first date, gutting it out.

Most anyone with actual talent will, over a long career, be characterized as "difficult"; how could it be otherwise?

I myself have, since the beginning of my career as a playwright, fifty years back, been castigated by the Eastern Cultural Bloc, which treated my work with sporadic, grudging acknowledgment, maturing through antipathy into loathing. But a man may be known, and perhaps known best, by his enemies. Is it not so?*

Many people, you may have noticed, are nuts. Many are lazy, or false, dreamy, unfeeling, manic, or some admixture of these—even as you and I. Some people, myself among them, are blessed to make a living employing the talents they were born with and improving on them to increase both enjoyment and gain.

---

\* "It's lonely at the top, but it ain't crowded." —*Speed-the-Plow*

Flying a helicopter is a learned skill. No one does it naturally, as it involves the sole menu of manipulations the human being wasn't born to accomplish navigation in three dimensions. Filmmaking is the practice and amalgamation of skills we've possessed since we climbed down from the trees to eat the fermented mangoes: direction of group efforts in construction, painting, clothing, movement, and so on. It is a sort of uber-choreography.

Now we come to acting, which, over the years, has become, to me, more and more of a mystery. Some folks out here speak of "the acting gene." This always seemed to me rather doltish, but I've come to believe that perhaps it's more accurate than not.

The basic skills involved in acting are all prosaic. They are the ability to speak clearly, to enunciate, to move purposefully (and gracefully, if possible), to hold still-but-not-immobile. These can be learned. And must be learned. The result of their acquisition may be a competent actor, one suitable only for set dressing, or a star.

Some actors can entrance us reading the phone book, others can send us off to nap-land while sharing magnificent dialogue or salacious scandal. The camera finds some faces fascinating and some opaque. And everybody wants to be in the movies.

I directed Gene Hackman in *Heist*. Time after time I'd call "action" and then hear him, it seemed, continuing his informal chat with another actor, as if he hadn't heard me. But he was, actually, playing the scene. There was no difference between his speech on-screen and off-, there was no added "help," or embellishment, or hieratic delivery.

I had the same experience directing John Malkovich. What were these fellows *doing*? They were acting. Could one learn to act like them? No. Or direct like Kubrick?

Where would we be without talent?

I must define it as that which cannot be defined, which is beyond both explanation and analysis. If it's not genetic, call me a moose. My god, it's grand to've been next to it.

# SINGING IN THE SHOWER

Consider Elvis, Nat King Cole, Billie Holiday, or Tony Bennett. They are, genetically, "sports" (like the albino tiger)—that is, unforeseeable and rare mutations.* They sing so naturally that we all know we can do likewise. As we can. But only in the shower.

For if someone is listening other than our most devoted fan, our pretentions will be revealed as false. We know we can't box like Mike Tyson and, should we be taken unaware, will encounter a natural corrective. But even should we have a shower companion, we know it would be a poor use of time to subject them to our warbling.

Dramatists, likewise, are "sports." Neither Shakespeare nor Johnny Mercer required a rhyming dictionary. Neither did Kipling. He made a grand poem out of the shipping news.

Dawn off the Foreland—the young flood making
   Jumbled and short and steep—
Black in the hollows and bright where it's breaking—
   Awkward water to sweep.
   "Mines reported in the fairway,
   "Warn all traffic and detain.
"'Sent up *Unity, Claribel, Assyrian, Stormcock,* and *Golden Gain.*"

---

\* *sport*: an animal, plant or part of a plant that shows an unusual or singular deviation from the parent type. *The Random House Dictionary of the English Language,* definition 12.

And Johnny Mercer made a song from the alexandrine he heard in a railroad's name: "On the Atchison, Topeka and the Santa Fe."

The Poet, the actual poet, does not think, What rhymes with "lutefisk"? He thinks in rhymes, that is, in the conjunction of two words, rather than in the completion of an idea through discovery of a similar sound.

Ted Morgan, in his biography, reports that Maugham, at dinner with Dorothy Parker, challenged her to write him a poem right then. She wrote:

Higgledy piggledy, my white hen.
She lays eggs for gentlemen.

She showed it to Maugham, he shrugged. She continued to write:

You cannot persuade her with gun or lariat
To come across for the proletariat.

One million monkeys at one million typewriters for one million years couldn't come up with it. Even with the aid of the rhyming dictionary.

Watch the comic onstage. He is heckled, and *watch* him, he will almost always respond, "*What* . . . ?" or "Say that again . . ."; and only after the reiteration will he come back with his quip. What was he doing in the interim? Was he "thinking"? Not in any sense that we would understand. He was, consciously or not, allowing some portion of his brain to catch up. You might ask him to review the process that led to his response, but there wasn't one. He's a genetic sport, and that's why he's onstage and we aren't. If he's overcome by the heckler, he's going to have to find another job. Who might hire him? The Studios.

Studio Executives are not The Audience, but a Committee of the Concerned. They understand their job as the application of

fiscal reason to the process of Creation. They are, in effect, the living rhyming dictionary, placed in power over their hireling, the writer.

In films, the talentless take an idea, that is, and search to see what matches with it. But they do not search their experience, but their *memory*. Of other films. We might understand a film displaying twenty "producers'" names, as their attempt to usurp credit; it is as accurate to suggest that they are trying to dilute blame.

Would we read a poem announcing a score of creators? The only songs crediting more than three, four at most, writers, included, in that list, the thieves and thugs.

Did Charlie Chaplin actually write "Smile"? Did Jolson write "Avalon"? Or were their credits a courtesy or an exaction? We can't know, but we can guess.

The actual artist just flat out sees things differently than his bureaucratic, neurotypical opponents. He is in league with that group they exist to exploit, the audience; and, so, of course the suits hate him. He needs them to get his cow to market, they need him for his cow, that is, his creativity—until it cannot be connected by the fatuous to their expectation of gain. At which point he is fired, the accepted Hollywood process, not taking his calls; and should a rationale be required for such brutishness, "screw him, he got paid." Which is sometimes true.

But there are those who have a debt to the form. What can that mean? Just as our friend The Beaver is driven mad by the sound of rushing water, a dramatic writer needs to complete or correct a composition until it's resolved. (In any case, I do.)

An example is *Suspicion*, starring Cary Grant as a bad 'un. He marries Joan Fontaine, but *is* he a thief, con man, and murderer, or not? Her suspicions are awakened, we always had ours; but the film will not resolve, and Hitch ends it sloppily, Cary's about to heave her out of a car, but at the last moment CHANGES HIS MIND, and they somehow live H. ever A. The audience must accept the ending, as there ain't no more. But we cannot enjoy it.

How, I wondered, over the years, *should* it end? What business was it of mine? The business I spent my life in.

My friend Lou Lenart (1921–2015) was a founder of the Israeli Air Force. We worked together on various films, and he invited me to Israel for a flight in an F-15. "Lou," I said, "you're sixty-five, why would they let you fly?" "It's my air force," he said.

The dramatically incorrect "nags me like an uncleaned gun." The correct composition gives me peace irrespective not only of its marketability but of its appeal to damn near anyone but myself. (General cries of, "Oh, my . . .") This is the Evil Twin of singing in the shower.

For example: Alaska has its Abominable Snowman, and New Jersey its own Favorite Son, that vicious swamp-dweller the Pine Barrens Devil. My idea for a book title: *The Pine Barrens Devil Redecorates: Papa's Got a Brand New Bog.*

On a less picayune note, my (current) favorite among my unproduced screenplays is *Russian Poland*.

Pre-Statehood members of the Haganah steal a British plane in Italy to fly to Israel. On the runway is an ancient DP, a displaced person, still wearing the striped rags of the Camps. They take him on board. During the flight he tells them stories to pass the time. They are the tales of Isaac Luria (1534–1572), the Ari (Lion) of Safed, a great Jewish Mystic. I set his stories in the nineteenth century, in the Pale of Settlement, the Russian Poland of my grandparents.

In my film the plane intermittently encounters difficulties, and the Old Man's arcane and Hasidic suggestions curiously aid the pilots. They are over Israel and, running on fumes, the pilot turns to the co-pilot and says, "Tell the old man to hang on, it's going to be a rough landing." The co-pilot looks, turns back, and says, "There's no one there."

That is the love of form in creation. Here's an example of correction. I love the arcana of war songs. We all know "Bless 'em all, /

Bless 'em all," but only those in the military realize the original lyrics contained a different verb.

"It's a long way to Tipperary" was famous as sung in the trenches—"It's the wrong way to tickle Mary"—and the most famous song of the Great War, "Mademoiselle from Armentières," not only did not suggest that she hadn't been *kissed* for a hundred years, it contained lyrics so filthy that none of them were ever transcribed. And so the interested would have to imagine them.

That is, more or less, what I've been doing as a dramatist.*

---

* One of my favorite Great War music hall songs: "The Rose of 'No Man's Land.'" My additions are the intro and the talk verse, highlighted in bold. I wrote them for my beloved Patti LuPone, who sang my version in concert. Am I a glutton for Appreciation? Who else goes into Show Business?

**Returned on Leave to England it sometimes fell by chance**
**That a curious Civilian asked after the boys in France.**
**There was little they could understand and less that I chose to tell**
**But I shared with them one circumstance which brightened our time in Hell.**

There's a rose that grows on "No Man's Land"
And it's wonderful to see,
Though it's sprayed with tears, it will live for years,
In my garden of memory.
It's the one red rose the soldier knows,
It's the work of the Master's hand;
'Mid the war's great curse stands the Red Cross Nurse,
She's the rose of "No Man's Land."

**The whistle blows and the troops retire but there's someone lingers beyond the wire.**
**When I close my eyes I can see the drape of dark gray dress and the scarlet cape.**
**To the end of my life I shall see it yet, as she looked from the edge of the parapet.**
**While she knelt and worked by the Trooper's side and she never left him until he died.**

There's a rose that grows on "No Man's Land"
And it's wonderful to see,
Though it's sprayed with tears, it will live for years,
In the garden of memory.
It's the one red rose the soldier knows,
It's the work of the Master's hand;
'Mid the war's great curse stands the Red Cross Nurse,
She's the rose of "No Man's Land."

# HOFFA

I was not fired off of *Hoffa*.

I was hired by Danny DeVito and Joe Roth, then head of 20th. I wrote the script and was called, as per usual, to take my beating. We were in a hotel on Central Park South (where I'd turned down *Once Upon a Time in America*), the above-named, and several Suits.

"Hi, hi, how was your trip can we get you anything, pause pause." And then one of the suits said, "I have some questions . . ." Joe interrupted and said, "*I* don't. Thank you." And they made the film.

Billy Wilder said that one must keep the first draft by him, as, sure as hell, he's going to come back to it.

Few films are better than the first draft, as subsequent diligence of an industrial committee always turns the thing into mush. The committee cannot improve a work of art.

The artist, asked, "Is it possible that everyone is wrong and you're right?" must answer, "It's *inevitable*"; the work was not produced by "everyone" but by an individual, who, if he possessed talent, had no objective other than pleasing himself.

I was left alone on *Hoffa*, and on *Ronin*, *The Verdict*, *The Postman Always Rings Twice*, *Wag the Dog*, and perhaps a few others.

I told the producers the story as I saw it, and they agreed, I wrote that story, and they shot it.

My pal Barb cut a film for a Very Famous Director. They went to preview screenings, and the director read each and every one of the comment cards, and asked Barb to recut the film according to them.

But not only were they generally foolish (What didn't you like?

The part where the villain shows up); they were, in bulk, contra-dictory.

A committee of producers, similarly, is made up of the foolish, the wise, the sycophantic, the cowed, and the arrogant. As in any meeting, a consensus may emerge. It is not a canvass, however it may be presented, but a direction from the He or She Wolf who has condescended to hear the counsel of inferiors.

Joe Roth *thanked* me for the *Hoffa* script. I am still stunned.

Danny, a prince, did a superb job—the phrase is insufficient.

My friend Ned Dowd was Danny's AD.

I was called from Boston to Hollywood to see the final cut. My father had just died, and I couldn't go. I called Ned, who'd seen it, and asked, "Is it any good?" And he said, "It's a masterpiece." I said, "Heh heh," and he said, "No, really." And I agree, it's clean as a hound's tooth.

I was with Danny, than whom no greater gentleman ever lived, in Montreal, shooting *Heist* with Becca Pidgeon and Gene Hackman. We often went out to dinner, preferring Queue de Cheval for the world's finest steaks and a lot of red wine.

One night we sat down, I saw a group of five or six at an ad-joining table. There were several beautiful women and a fellow in his forties—a tough-looking, obvious thug. He recognized Danny. Dinner was served, and the man came over and mentioned his name, which nobody caught, and said he'd be honored if we came to his table for a cognac. Danny said, "No, thank you." Back-and-forth. Danny said, "Thank you, really, no." The fellow said, "You don't know who I *am*." And Danny said, "I don't give a fuck who you are. Get lost." God bless him.

We were shooting the big shootout on the dock. Becca has ratted out her lover, Gene, to Danny, his archrival; Gene and Delroy Lindo have it out with Dan and his hidden sharpshooters, and at one point Danny starts shouting his (my) dialogue to his cohorts (I can't recall it offhand), ending his speech, "I COULD SAY THIS SHIT *ALL DAY*."

Joe Roth was head of 20th Century Fox till 1993. I wished someone would have asked me to comment on the reasons for his retirement, as my prepared response was, "He only has seven years to come up with a new company name, and he couldn't stand the pressure."

# COURAGE AND HYPOCRISY

Why should one look for courage among the movie stars, they're just human. And, like the rest of us, generally turn peevish before inconvenience, arrogant in success, and cowardly before challenge.

Movie folk love proximity to actual heroism—the Farthest Left opponent of the police (in neighborhoods other than his own) will fawn over the cops and the military advisors on his films.

There are ample opportunities for persistence in moviemaking, but few for courage. But there are a few. The star who refuses to do a pornographic sequence called a "love scene" may have to stand up to The Man; the character actress who does so may get fired.

Diversity is well and good; it is no more foolish than Francis the Talking Mule, and, like that oeuvre, will at some point die of its own absurdity. It is like Modern Art, where the object is not superior to a description of itself. My daughter went to New York and saw, at MoMA, a violin, stuffed with corn. Get it? You wouldn't get it to a greater degree by seeing it at MoMA.

"Diversity" is presented as "any person can and should be allowed to play any part"; an Asian man playing Ève Curie may be considered foolish or provocative (mealy-mouthed for "foolish"), but a white man playing Dr. King would be objectionable. This being the case, what is diversity? The above example reveals it as the usurpation of power, the newly powerful those who can insist on acceptance of their own definitions.

In an old-style love scene between a man and a woman, gays and straights could choose the object of their fantasy. In the same-team films, one group is debarred from doing so. Further, in old films, the odds were good that one of the stars kissing was actually lesbian or gay, a knowledge (or the rumors) of which were certainly in that gay community. Gays, that is, could fantasize about their like not only in the nonsexual scenes but also in the clinches, for his or her team member's ability to put it over on the straights.

An overwhelming percentage of actors have always been gay. Film was a community shielded from outside meddling by the power of the studios. They'd protect their investment from the Puritans by co-opting the press and the cops. Unless the investment proved troublesome, in which case it was ratted out and/or framed. See the Roscoe Arbuckle case, where a now failing star was accused of raping a prostitute to death (she actually died of peritonitis); the harassment of Lizabeth Scott, hounded as a "pervert," that is, lesbian; the magnificent Jean Seberg, who had the FBI sicced on her for consorting with the Black Panthers in Paris; and Robert Mitchum, who did a jolt for being found with a joint at some party. Who sent the cops there?

It's a rough business indeed, and those seeking justice may find it in the dictionary. Sometimes the rabbit wins, and sometimes the dog wins. And each man, in his time, plays many parts. If O. J. had been a little neater in his entertainment, he'd have been allowed to walk away without the inconvenience of a trial.

My friend Steve, a stuntman, got run over on the set. No one was held accountable. He was "shot dead," and was to fall by the wheels of the parked getaway car, the film's star in the driver's seat. The director yelled "cut," and the star, for some reason, thought it good to put the car in reverse, and run over Steve. He was extracted after an hour and spent more than a year recovering. The star was whisked away from set, and never even questioned.

My friend Buddy is a stunt coordinator. He's had to stand up to various directors insisting on hurrying the stunt prep up, disregarding time- or money-consuming safety measures; and, recently, insisting on diversity in casting stuntfolk who, though fitted by genetics and skill, are unfitted for the stunt at hand.

Joi "SJ" Harris, an African American motorcycle rider, was hired to do a stunt, as SAG insisted the stuntperson must duplicate the actor she was doubling. The actor was a Black woman, so the rider must be, too. A search could find no Black female stuntwoman motorcycle rider. There was a Black stuntman, the same size as the actress, but he was unacceptable. There was a white woman stuntrider, but she too was a no-go. The Black stuntman and the white stuntwoman could have done the gag in makeup, but the Union said no, and Joi Harris was found. She'd won many motorcycle races, but she'd never done a stunt. And she didn't complete the one she was hired for. The director called "action," and she started riding down the steps, as per the script, lost control, and died. Who would take the blame for the poor woman's death? The Diversity Committee? Don't make me laugh.

What of actual courage in films?

*The Picture of Dorian Gray* (1945) stars Hurd Hatfield, a very handsome young man. Gray, you remember, stays forever young, all his sins transferred to his portrait, which is hidden in the attic. It is one of Wilde's masterpieces and quite clearly a comment upon unending sexual profligacy fighting the sad decay of age.

Wilde's arena was a crypto-depiction of his Gay London, and Hurd's performance was of an androgynous young beauty. Hatfield wrote that he was so successful in the part that it was difficult for him to be cast otherwise. But he can be seen, in a great performance, as a gay man in Richard Fleischer's *The Boston Strangler*. Henry Fonda, playing the investigator, finds a lead suggesting the Strangler might be gay. He goes to a gay nightclub and sees Hatfield there at the bar.

It becomes clear that they knew each other, or knew of each other, in college (we may assume Harvard). Hatfield says, "What brought you here, the Old School Tie . . . ?" He asks why Fonda is harrying the folks in the club, and Fonda responds with a gay slur. Hatfield keeps his composure and says that he is disappointed in Fonda, as he thought better of him. Fonda takes a moment and apologizes sincerely. He says he regrets the remark, and is most sorry. Hatfield replies, "I believe you actually are."

There's courage in Hatfield taking the openly gay role in 1968, and there's courage in Fonda, who delivers both the slur and the subsequent apology without reserve. These uncurated human interactions—on stage and screen—leave a viewer *improved*. This is not deference to, or a depiction of, courage but an example of it.

As is Dirk Bogarde's performance in *Victim*, as the closeted, married, successful barrister who's being blackmailed for his homosexuality. He finally decides to go to the police, at the cost of his career.

Playing the part was an act of courage on the part of Bogarde, a gay man, and of those playing his friends, many of whom were gay.

Wilde went to prison not for his homosexuality but for a quip. He was interrogated about his supposed (and then illegal) homosexuality and was doing fine on the stand, charming all, until asked if he had kissed a particular bellboy. "Oh, dear, no," he said. "He was a peculiarly plain boy."

All of the court, defense and prosecution, and judges, had been to Public Schools and Oxbridge and had participated in or functioned in an atmosphere of gay life. (Cf. the designation LTC, lesbian till commencement, universal currency at the Seven Sisters colleges.)

No one in Wilde's court, gay or not, was unaware that homosexuality was not only practiced and tolerated but, in some slices of some circles, understood as a superior lifestyle. Wilde spent two years in prison not for sexual practices but for flaunting the taboo requiring hypocrisy.

It's the function of comedy to mock hypocrisy and that of current drama to celebrate it.

If the motorcycle rider actually must replicate the race and sex of the actress—even at the cost of her life—why not demand certificates of homosexuality from those portraying gays, a diagnosis of tuberculosis from anyone playing Camille, and death certificates from the cast of *When We Dead Awaken*?

These demands and their outrageous like are the protected committee version of Activism, but where is the committee member who, on his eventual indictment, did not plead ignorance of his group's depredations or point to his responsibility to Just Follow Orders?

I did a cartoon advertising "Now Playing, Roy Rogers, King of the Cowboys, in": the rest of the image obscured by a banner posted across (a "snipe"), its message "TRIGGER WARNING!!!" I love the cartoon, but no one younger than sixty gets it. Trigger was, as the old folks know, the name of Roy Rogers's horse.

Roy's real name was Leonard Slye, a fellow from Cincinnati. He and his partner and wife, Dale Evans, made the most popular Westerns, and then television shows, of the mid-century. But their fame, as all fame, has vanished 'neath the sands of time that also buried my cartoon.

But I do know of a few trigger warnings.

Bad Seed Youth of today have forsaken panty raids, and illicit smoking, for screaming if someone "hurts their feelings." Idiot adults go along with the gag, which, naturally, frightens the children, encouraging more screaming.

But there is a use for trigger warnings. They may be used to warn us of drivel. Here are some telltale clues: Any movie having an "overture"; any variation of "based on a True Story"; a list of four or more "Producers" in the Head Titles; and the credit ". . . and introducing . . ." No one given that credit ever was seen again. You, my reader, may have counterexamples; I do not.

Here are Nelson Algren's trigger warnings: "never play cards with a man called Doc, never eat at a place called Mom's, and never sleep with a woman whose troubles are worse than your own,"* to which I've added the invaluable "never trust a Jew in a bow tie."

---

* *A Walk on the Wild Side* (1956).

Algren, also, sacrificed precision for a quip. For how would one know if a woman's problems were worse than one's own? How would a woman know if a man's were? Is the camouflage of these not the essence of courting?

And now businesspeople have ceased wearing "office attire," and few wear ties either horizontal or vertical. The wider Western world adopts the motto "Never Trust a Jew," in any case, but exercises a nonprejudiced graciousness in extending their trust, in times of need, to doctors, lawyers, accountants, and so on, of my religion. Thus Hitler may in fact have *weakened* his influence by identifying the Jews. The yellow star meaning, to the Germans, "Do your *own* fricking taxes . . ."

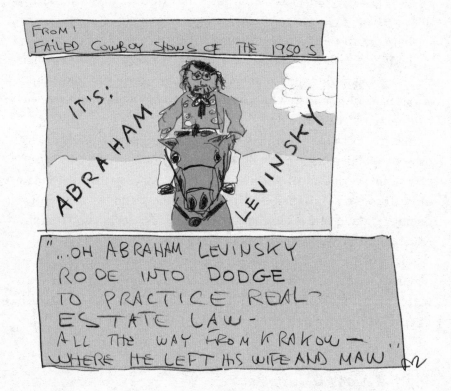

If everything in our modern and connected lives must "do good," what time and energy have we set aside with which to enjoy ourselves?

The performance of virtue, we have all noted, always is accompanied by a self-satisfied expression never found at a square dance, poker tournament, or demolition derby.

# HISTORY

The study of history can be reduced to the simple phrase: "What the hell happened?"

Our ability to connect cause and effect definitively is small.

An event may be grasped from different perspectives, with differing access to information; the information itself may be false or incomplete and certainly will, at best, be tainted by the bias, conscious or not, of the observer.

Autobiography, a particularly tainted form of history, must always be discounted as the work of the self-obsessed. This is true of all jailhouse tell-alls, where the writer will admit to any but the most horrific of crimes, ascribing those to Jimmy or Moose, the writer himself looking on aghast.

Psychoanalysis is the purchase from a warped observer (committed to his own theories) of a moot account. It is very much a form of contact mind reading. Here the blindfolded magician holds the hand of an audience member and leads him to the Hidden Object. It's explained that the Blindfolded Seer holds the fellow's hand to keep him from bumping into things, but of course it is the audience member who is unconsciously leading the performer.

Like all magic tricks and illusions, this is dismaying when revealed; for we then learn it is not the performer who was supplying the magic but we ourselves. We who allow the waving of a magic wand to relieve us of boring knowledge that a rabbit was not actually pulled out of a hat, that we've been induced to lead ourselves to that conclusion. The wand freed us of the knowledge that the beast came, and could only have come, out of a hat that *only appeared to be empty* and which in fact contained a rabbit.

A true, which is to say useful, understanding of history must func-
. tion like an analysis of a magic trick. a) What *did I actually see*?
(What historical reports can reasonably be accounted accurate?);
b) What must have been the conditions predicate? (What can I reasonably accept as facts which might have led to the reported event?)
History thus is like Freud's understanding of psychoanalysis as "the
art of the obvious."

John Wilkes Booth shot Abraham Lincoln in Ford's Theatre. He then
leapt to the stage and shouted, "*Sic semper tyrannis.*"

He was a second-rate actor, the younger brother of Edwin Booth,
the most famous of contemporary thespians.

But in leaping to the stage and declaiming, John Wilkes became
*literally* the most famous actor ever to've trod the stage. He is the
direct progenitor of generations of performers who misuse the spot-
light to assert the superiority of their political views.

In 2007, the Writers Guild of America went on strike against the
studios, demanding higher DVD residuals and residuals for New
Media, which is to say pie-in-the-sky. The strike failed, thousands
of folk were driven out of work (among them those on my television show *The Unit*—pre-strike, twelve million viewers a week;
post-strike, goose egg).

The Guild (of which I was, and believe I still am, a member) demanded writers march on the picket line, which led me to the only
cartoon I sold to the *Los Angeles Times*.

I was asked by members of my own writers' staff to picket. I told
them they were out of their minds to strike. I got hate mail from
those I'd employed—indeed *discovered*—suggesting I was a less than
admirable fellow.

During the fourteen-week-long strike, the Guild instituted "teach-
ing Thursdays" on the picket line. Here the class-conscious "workers" convened study groups on the history of the Labor Movement,
of their gallant forebears, and of the construction of plot—this last

knowledge moot, as most of the self-dispossessed never worked again. Their jobs were eliminated by the studios, who saw the wisdom of sidelining union members and their funny ways. The studios wiped out hours of Dramatic Programming, replacing it with "Reality Shows," which hired not writers but "editors" (writers who weren't in the union).

The striking writers, like the actors, were too close to a fantasy—in their case, worker solidarity in the face of oppression.

The truest wisdom is that of the poker game, "Don't play 'em if you don't got 'em." And the striking writers' foes were two: the studios; and the strikers' out-of-work brethren (the vast majority of Guild members), happy, by voting, to participate once again in the entertainment—powerful, if only as destroyers.

Did the studios oppress the workers? Well, they *hired* them.

I came up with a gag, some time back, but never got the correct film in which to use it.

We come to the obligatory soft-music/hard-extremities "love" scene. The music assures the audience they have not waited in vain. We see two bodies, moving, sinuous, so close we cannot determine which is which. The music swells, the camera pulls back to reveal we're watching a couple of eels.

A friend of mine, a very famous actor, told me he was doing a "love" scene with the female star. He was wearing the flesh-colored cache-sexe, meant to prohibit actual intromission. The scene ended, he saw he'd lost the device, and he said to his co-star, "I beg your pardon: was I fucking you?"

It's a long way from Tipperary.

And since we've descended to bawdy.

A fellow director was flying to New York to see Rex Harrison—that nonbinding politeness called "offer of a part, subject to a meeting."

Rex was appearing on Broadway with Claudette Colbert. My friend had to make the curtain, but his plane was late arriving.

He jumped into a cab at LaGuardia, and told the driver, Forty-Fifth and Broadway, here's a hundred bucks if you make it before the eight o'clock curtain.

The driver pulled out and floored it. There they went.

The driver said, Where you going?

My friend said, To see *Aren't We All*.

Driver: Who's in it?

My friend: Rex Harrison and Claudette Colbert.

The driver pulled over, put it in park, and turned to my friend. "Claudette Colbert?" he said. "Claudette *Colbert* . . . ? I FUCKED HER MAID!"

Are these examples too coarse?

The military teaches that one can assess the quality of a new command by three things: morale, esprit de corps, and humor.

If those three are present, the command is healthy. If not, not.

# THE FLOCKY

Shakespeare told us there is a destiny that shapes our ends. Kim Kardashian sought out a different aesthetician, and Gloria Grahame was obsessed, for some reason, about her upper lip. She went under the knife several times to have it altered.

A joke from the dawn of liposuction was that the doctors saved the material they extracted from one patient to inject into another wanting augmentation; one might think he were kissing Ursula Andress's lips, but one was actually kissing Dom DeLuise's ass.

Gloria married the stepson of her husband Nick Ray. Greer Garson married the young actor playing her son in *Mrs. Miniver*. Celebrity confuses people. When many are clamoring for our opinions, we forget that we have nothing to say. We speak and, as we are celebrities, believe that our speeches from the podium are other than platitudes or nonsense. Politicians are narcissists, they are doing it on purpose to control, but we showfolk come by our self-absorption in two stages. First, knowing or thinking ourselves beautiful or funny, we elbow our way or are dragged into the limelight. Then, as the nice fans are smiling at our blather, we conclude we're smart.

Our work as writers consists largely in delivering platitudes or nonsense to the Industry. In publicity we will not abandon that proven formula.

Brad Pitt announced that he is quitting show business. But what is that announcement but a bid for notoriety, the sequel being the inevitable announcement of his decision to return?

Causes and Good Works are nothing but publicity. The excellent person does good anonymously—Jewish wisdom is that the highest *tzedakah* (righteousness, often mistranslated as "charity") is for neither the benefactor nor the recipient to know the other's identity.

I was in a bar in London years ago at "Oscar Time." That lovefest was on the telly. One of the drinkers said, "Why are they strutting about like that for a statue, don't we pay them enough . . . ?" In the '80s, I commuted regularly to London to see my girl. She was starring at the National Theatre and cutting her records for Polygram. I spent my time in her apartment either waiting for her return or trying to make her late for work.

We were friendly with the Pythons (Monty). Their film company office, Prominent Features, was just down the block. They graciously offered me a room to work in. One January I came down with pneumonia. Becca went to rehearsal, and I dragged myself down the block every day to the Pythons' office and went to sleep on the office floor.

I'm a near-plank owner of Second City (founded in 1959; I worked there as a busboy in 1964). All its imitators are to me as chaff, whatever chaff is. But there was a simultaneous flowering of magnificence at Oxbridge, Dudley Moore, Peter Cook, Jonathan Miller, and Alan Bennett, improvising College Humor. (Michael O'Donoghue, of the *Lampoon* and *Saturday Night Live*, said, "'Sophomoric' is asshole for 'funny.'") Pete and Dud broke new Wind. Followed immediately by The Pythons. W. C. Fields said of Bert Williams that he was the funniest man he'd ever seen. And the saddest. He would have said the same of John Cleese.

Pythons to one side, as the Brits say, what of *Fawlty Towers*? Twelve sitcom episodes about a mismanaged inn. They were written by John and Connie Booth. They are unforgettable. John told me he'd expanded the idea into a company training folks for the Hospitality Industry. This, to me, was genius.

Where is the sane writer who didn't scheme to turn his essays into a book, his diary entries into a memoir—in short, to use every part of the Pig?

Ricky Jay always kvetched that he could figure out no way to make money while he slept. He was available for Private Gatherings, at an insufficiently large fee. Booked by his manager, Winston Simone.

Winston, Ricky, Bex, and I went to some TV show Rix and I were doing. Milton Berle, our 1950s Uncle Miltie, was on ahead of us. He came offstage and introductions were exchanged. "Winston Simone?" he said. "Any relation to Simone Simone, only woman who ever gave me the clap . . . ?"

Milton was famous for his outsize genitalia. Two men at the Friars Club made bets on the length. Uncle Miltie was asleep on a massage table, covered by a towel. The men went in and explained their errand. The fellow who'd bet high said, "Milton, just take out enough to win."

There are, of course, inevitable versions of this story. I've heard it told about Forrest Tucker and, more recently, about a magnificently endowed actor playing Christ. There he was, expiring, stark naked, on the Cross, and filming was brought to a standstill by the Centurion's line "*Truly* He is the Son of God."

It was a randy business.

But nothing can be amusing that is prefaced "This may not be politically correct, *but . . .*"

The Friars Club Roasts were notorious for their obscenity. (Someone said, of discussion of some fading star, "I wouldn't fuck her with Bea Arthur's dick.") By way of segue, these Clubs offered the camaraderie that made the poor illusion of "humanitarian" communion-with-the-audience unnecessary.

The best segue of all, Alan King's. First joke finishes, he adjusts his tie, says, "No, but I gotta say . . ." and begins next joke.

I thought Cleese's double-dipping both legitimate and charming (trans: moneymaking).* So I rummaged through my work and came up with an idea. All salespeople, it seems, know my play *Glengarry Glen Ross*. How's about, I thought, if I sent my imaginary critters out on the street to bring me back some money in "Salesmanship Seminars"?

But I was spared, I tell you, by what Mercy of the Fates I ken not,

---

* Was Cleese not more worthy than I? Yes. He not only was funny, but he looked smashing in a dress, while my attempts at Drag are a grand endorsement for cisgenderism.

but aren't they like that? One spins, one weaves, and one cuts the thread. The Wise, that is, legitimately chastened, man must look back not only grateful for his blessings but, more, awed by the shames he was, incomprehensibly, spared.

I did not sell my brand for a mess of pottage, but it was not for lack of effort.

God, we are told, always answers our prayers, but sometimes the answer is no. God bless 'im.

Was I arrogant in my fifty years in Show Biz? You bet.

But only toward my inferiors.

These were not the actors, the crew, or the audience.

A wiser man might have Gone Further if he had learned not humility but diplomacy. I am not a wiser man. But I am a lucky one.

Ancients, religious and savage, interdicted the utterance of the name of God. Modern agnostics unwittingly do the same, substi-

tuting "Nature," "The Universe," or even "the way things are." But a Higher Power spared me not from all but, to date, from various unbearable acts of Hubris, awarding me a Flocky.

What is a Flocky?

Mrs. Greenberg and Mrs. Schwartz meet at the Mahjong Club. Mrs. Schwartz has a small cast on her wrist. She explains it is a Flocky.

Mrs. Goldberg asks what that means.

Mrs. Schwartz: I was coming downstairs and tripped. I fell all the way down. The doctor examined me and said I'd only sprained my wrist. He said, "You got a flocky."

# BACKWASH

What did it all mean, what can it all have meant: that I know the *Maltese Falcon* statue appears in a second film, *Conflict* (1945), Bogey here playing a wife-killer. He's called in by the cops and some hip set decorator has placed The Falcon in the cop's bookcase, behind Bogey's head.

His nemesis is proved to be Sydney Greenstreet, playing straight as a crime-solving psychologist. Bogey did five films with Greenstreet. Of them, *The Maltese Falcon* and *Casablanca* both featured Peter Lorre, also of their rep company. A retired cop friend told me that Lorre's daughter, Catharine, was stopped on Mulholland by Angelo Buono and Kenneth Bianchi, the killers then known co-jointly as the Hillside Strangler, terror of L.A. in the seventies. The Stranglers took her purse and were going to off her when one saw her driver's license. "He's my father," she said, and they let her off as a sort of Professional Courtesy.

Lorre was one of my folk, a Jew, who escaped from the Nazis and fetched up in my neighborhood on the Westside, in sight of the Pacific Ocean.

I've always found the Pacific Ocean a bore.

I was raised on Lake Michigan and lived most of my life on the Atlantic, two notably various bodies of water. I know the Pacific gets rambunctious just a bit from shore, but I only see it from the shore, and as an ocean it disappoints.

The Jewish actors moved out here to save their lives, leaving behind not only great careers in Europe (Lorre, Conrad Veidt, Hedy Lamarr,

Marcel Dalio, Paul Lukas, and on and on) but their world, which is to say their culture. And here one finds oneself now, the film and theatrical culture of the twentieth century dead. As the means of distribution have been superseded.

No one goes to Broadway save tourists, who want tourist fare, and that's not only comprehensible but inevitable. Nineteenth-century tourists to Italy may have found actual Etruscan artifacts, unappreciated in this or that remote village; later, pilgrims in search of Art were sold bogus masterpieces in Florence and Rome, and the Religious for two thousand years have always brought home guaranteed fragments of the True Cross. Today in Rome the streets are filled with shops hawking plaques of the genitals of Michelangelo's David, the wise shopper given the choice of various penis colors and lengths.

Universal Studios makes a fortune having transformed its lot, where films were made, into a nostalgia/amusement park, a financially canny use of the land. The fungible backflow: not only millions paying to go "Eek" at Jurassic Park monsters but the creation of a dedicated audience identified as conditioned to buy anything that makes it go "Eek."

I know of old, from my days in the Boiler Room, selling this or that over the telephone, that the best lead is that which took the sucker time. He or she who actually cut the ad out of a magazine and mailed it in with a return address is demanding to be screwed. And, financially best-of-all, the folks at Universal have the credit card info of attendees, who will no doubt receive all sorts of Special Offers upon their return home.

The Hillside Stranglers let Ms. Lorre off, but Universal will use every part of the pig but the squeal. The success of the amusement park has inevitably affected the remaining movies actually produced. For the folks queue up for the roller coaster to go "Whee" for a few seconds over a ten-minute ride, and the same progression and percentage are found in the tentpole—producers and consumers both understanding that the product is a legitimate number of thrills separated by just-bearable filler.

Nothing wrong with that, unless one happens to be a writer; for the thrills will be created by the blue screen folk, independent of the script, and the fill is all generic, requiring a dramatist not at all. The screenwriter, once a scenarist, is here exactly like his primordial brethren, the writers-of-titles for the silents.

They wrote "Night Fell Swiftly on the Tropics," a useless explanation of the shot of a sunset; and today's flacks craft dialogue, commenting on the same shot, "Well, Jim, sun's up, I guess that means we'd better be ridin'."

I spent several afternoons with Lauren Bacall (née Perske). Her house had been flooded out or something, and she was living in a cottage at the Bel-Air, then the world's greatest hotel. The studios put me up there when I was in town working on a film. And there I sat, every afternoon, at the pool, in a lounge chair, writing, and taxed with lifting an eyebrow whenever I needed a pool boy to come by and bring me something to eat or drink. And we chatted, Miss Bacall and I, about this and that.

She'd been the childhood friend, in New York, of my friend Andy Potok. His family was friendly with the Perskes; Andy and their Betty were pals. I never got the courage to call Miss Bacall "Betty."

Andy, a friend in Vermont for fifty years, was a painter. He went blind, in his thirties, from retinitis pigmentosa, and he began to write. His memoir *Ordinary Daylight* is a masterpiece. He asked me to adapt it for a film. I wrote the screenplay, and some producer gave it to Penny Marshall. Penny said she'd make it (joy all around), but she had a few notes on the script. She gave it to some slave and asked her to highlight those parts of the book that didn't make it into the screenplay. I went to a meeting and Penny handed me the book, with everything highlighted save the prepositions. I bet the producer five grand that she wouldn't make the film within six months, he took the bet, and at the conclusion of the stated period, he replied, to my request for the cash, "I was just fooling." Andy can be seen as one of the poker players in my film *House of Games*. Others include Bob and Al, other members of my Vermont Poker Game, and Ricky Jay.

Ricky and I mapped out a screenplay based upon an Oscar scam. Lord, how I miss Ricky. What didn't he know?

As all aerobatic maneuvers are only different arrangements of the loop and the roll, all con games are essentially the inculcation of greed, coupled with misdirection—the pigeon drop ("Oh, look, is this your wallet?") essentially identical to the Great Housing Bubble ("Would you like this house for nothing?"). And so, we looked at the Oscars, saddened that *House of Games*, written by me, inspired by him, had not been named best picture of the decade.

He grew up doing the Bally in a carnival,* and I on the South Side and on the edge of various questionable endeavors. Well, then, we reasoned of the Oscars, as we have certainly suffered not only loss but treachery (were that year's judges suborned or only blind?), why not spin the flax to gold and do a film about stealing the Oscars?

One, two, six, as they said, and the answer, as in Magic and Aerobatics, presented itself as the inevitable combination of one or two basics.

There has existed since the days of the world's second horse a surefire method to profit from a horse race that depended not at all on the animal's performance. The racetrack tout (one who sells tips) merely had to circulate in the crowd and sell his knowledge of the Sure Winner. Easy to do. With nine horses running, he only required nine suckers. He sold each one on a different horse, and one of the suckers of course won. And here is the beauty part, he then *came back. For more.*

Q. How do you inflame the greed of the horseplayers?

A. You sell them a sure thing.

Now: Why should they believe you had the ability to pick a winner?

A. As you just *did* so. (He was the one sure winner of the nine— he is now hooked.)

The tout at first must answer the sucker's eternal and essential question: Why me? The tout's explanation: As it costs you little.

---

* "They're on the inside, folks, they're on the *inside . . .*"

Or, indeed, nothing. He can even say, "I'll give you the first winner for nothing, and you split the winnings with me when you find I'm right." The sucker is set up. He comes back and says, "Tell me the winner in the next race," and *now* the con man shakes him down. ("Pay me.")

In our film, the con men (Rix and Bex) sell a producer with a nominated film this story: when the Oscar envelope is passed to the Presenter, no one knows the winner's name *save* the Accountancy Firm and the presenter who opens the envelope. If the wrong name is read, the accountants would be unlikely to blow the whistle on their flawed security; all one has to do is to bribe the guy who opens the envelope. The con men find out who that particular presenter will be, and do a bit of legwork. They are looking for his particular exploitable *troubles*: sexual, financial, familiar. Here they employ the same ancient technique of the stickup artist. In the days before everyone wore a mask, the stickup guy pasted some adhesive tape over one temple, painted as if seeping blood or pus (you see, you are already turning away). *That* is what the bank teller remembered. So in *our* case, we told this tale: the Star to be suborned was paying off a blackmailer (that's why he needs the money), and the sucker's attention was distracted from the tale's implausability, and drawn to the salacious.

How did our heroes impress the mark with their proximity to the Star? They confessed that *they* were the blackmailers. Pretty good.

They figured, they said, that they could actually get more money through bribing the Star and fixing the Oscars than by shaking him down. Now the sucker is distracted by the proximity to a scandal in which he *must* believe, for the blackmailers have confessed themselves criminals. They have given him *their* confidence. The two basic principles of Magic are here, 1) anticipation—the trick is accomplished before the mark knows it is in operation; 2) misdirection—as the scam progresses, the mark is distracted by difficulties in the Star's itinerary: he was supposed to receive the bribe in Pasadena, but he changed his plans; he has drunk himself sick from fear of exposure, and so on.

The sucker's attention now is not on the confidence folk but on the Star. At the racetrack the anticipation is the selling of the First

Tip; by the time the sucker comes back to plead for another go, the trick is already accomplished. The misdirection will come after the score; while the mark is waiting for his Final Winner to romp home, the touts are far, far away. The punch line to our script was that Bex and Rix, having taken the mark for five mil to fix the Oscars, wonder how to expand their operations, and decide to "fix" a Presidential Election.

Someone is stealing my material.

Our Oscar film was going apace, as part of the usual transSiberian railway journey of Idea to Screen; and then the rumor spread that someone had stolen the gag FOR REAL. You may have heard that some woman was nominated for a Best Supporting Actress award; and the Presenter was Her Best Friend, who opened the envelope and spoke a name that may, in fact, not have been written on the card. A superb bit of film lore, and we all, of course, hope it was true. As, film producers' understanding to the contrary, we all love a good story.

How, Rix and I wondered, could The World be so cruel as to ruin our grand idea? Here is the answer: we say that such and such is unthinkable only of those things that have just been thought of—fantasized by ourselves or accomplished by others.*

There's a lot of world out there; and there are a lot of people, you and I included, scheming on its more gainful exploitation. The grand perception of psychoanalysis, for the dramatist, is that all actions are performed FOR A REASON, and that one may reason backward from the action, however absurd or self-destructive, to a

---

\* My first play in New York was *Sexual Perversity in Chicago*. Some producers bought the rights, fucked up the script (an act of vandalism), and then CHANGED THE TITLE (an act of insanity).

Three years after it came out, as *About Last Night*, Steven Soderbergh brought out *Sex, Lies, and Videotape*. I don't recall the film, but I do recall the title, the salacious power of which would have/should have been mine.

Years later Soderbergh commissioned me to write a Dillinger script. I wrote a lulu, and he shitcanned it and made another film, a piece of crap. An odd choice.

cause. The determination may be arbitrary, or indeed wrong, but it may be made. Further, that, for the dramatist, the process may be reversed, the cause postulated first, and its development to a conclusion graphed—at which point (in the tragedy only; and in the drama previously) the cause of the progression is clear.

The dramatist as analyst, unfortunately, cannot punch out and go home. The psychoanalyst can leave his work at the office (the old saw being that if you were introduced at the cocktail party as an analyst, you had to put up with being told, "Oh, now I suppose you can read my thoughts . . . so I must be careful . . ."). No, the Doctor can happily walk away from his bread-and-butter tales of woe. But the dramatist has no off button. All human behavior, to him, is either

a revelation or a confirmation. Of what? Of human variations on the themes of sin and folly.

Which I introduce in reference to the Oscars, and the reality of their potential for subversion. What could have brought this to mind (my own and Ricky's, or the nominee's Best Friend's)? I suggest it was the ritual insistence, every year, upon their absolute security.

The French between the wars built the impregnable Maginot Line to defend against the Germans. The Germans looked at a map, saw where the Maginot Line ended, and attacked *there*.

How do we know the Oscars can be fixed? *Everything* can be fixed. This is the lesson we can take from the magicians: the more intelligent one is, the easier he is to fool. Magic invites the observer to let his intelligence lead him to its overthrow. Just like Dramatists. When we are doing our job. When we are not, we're merely writing propaganda; not even *Francis the Talking Mule* but "Francis the Talking Mule Rids Himself of Prejudice."

# L'ENVOI

Billy Friedkin told me he'd improvised the car chase in *The French Connection*. Peter Yates told me he'd improvised the car chase in *Bullitt*. John Frankenheimer told me he'd improvised the car chase in *Ronin*, and the fantasy/brainwashing scenes in *The Manchurian Candidate*. Mike Nichols told me that Ingrid Bergman was a Jew and Gloria Steinem a CIA spy. Dorothy Gish told me that Mr. Griffith didn't lay a finger on her or her sister, Lillian, during *Orphans of the Storm*. James Jones's widow, Gloria, told me she was the leg stand-in for Marilyn Monroe. Mary Steenburgen told me she never slept with Jack Nicholson on *Goin' South*. I believed them all.

# ACKNOWLEDGMENTS

With thanks to Pam Susemiehl, David Vigliano, Robert Messenger, and the editors and staff at Simon & Schuster.

# INDEX

# ABOUT THE AUTHOR

DAVID MAMET received the Pulitzer Prize for his 1984 play *Glengarry Glen Ross*. He has written and directed ten films, including *Homicide, The Spanish Prisoner, State and Main, House of Games, Spartan,* and *Redbelt*. His screenplays for *The Verdict* and *Wag the Dog* were nominated for Academy Awards.